Match Yourself with the Perfect Job

COURTING YOUR CAREER

SHAWN GRAHAM, M.Ed.

JIST Works
America's Career Publisher

Courting Your Career

© 2008 by Shawn Graham

Published by JIST Works, an imprint of JIST Publishing
7321 Shadeland Station, Suite 200
Indianapolis, IN 46256-3923
Phone: 800-648-JIST   Fax: 877-454-7839   E-mail: info@jist.com

Visit our Web site at **www.jist.com** for information on JIST, free job search tips, book chapters, and ordering instructions for our many products!

Quantity discounts are available for JIST books. Have future editions of JIST books automatically delivered to you on publication through our convenient standing order program. Please call our Sales Department at 800-648-5478 for a free catalog and more information.

Trade Product Manager: Lori Cates Hand
Copy Editor: Chuck Hutchinson
Interior Designer: Marie Kristine Parial-Leonardo
Cover Designer: Trudy Coler
Cover Illustrator: Philip Brooker
Cartoonist: Kevin H. Dixon
Proofreaders: Paula Lowell, Jeanne Clark
Indexer: Joy Dean Lee

Printed in the United States of America
12 11 10 09 08 07   9 8 7 6 5 4 3 2 1

  Library of Congress Cataloging-in-Publication Data
Graham, Shawn, 1973-
  Courting your career : match yourself with the perfect job / Shawn Graham.
      p. cm.
  Includes index.
  ISBN 978-1-59357-512-0 (alk. paper)
1. Job hunting. I. Title.
  HF5382.7.S72 2008
  650.14--dc22

2007031775

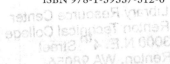

About This Book

You're not that attractive. Don't get me wrong; I'm sure you're a very nice person. It's just that there's probably someone out there who is better looking, in better shape, or who has a lot more money than you. That's just the way it is. But does that stop you from dating? I seriously hope not. The same holds true when you're looking for a great job. There's always going to be someone out there with better grades, with more experience, with more whatever. To attain the unattainable, whether it's a hot guy or girl, or a high-paying job with the corner office, you must outshine your competition. This book is designed to help you do just that by drawing parallels between your dating experience and your job search.

What do they really have in common? When you get right down to it, they both involve our search for relationships. After all, choosing a mate and choosing a career are two of the biggest decisions we make in life. And the similarities don't end there. In both cases, we want to be liked and want others to like us. We need to know what we have to offer someone and what that person has to offer us. We need to differentiate ourselves from other singles or job applicants on the market.

Through my years as a career counselor working at both the University of North Carolina at Chapel Hill and at Westminster College, I have seen undergraduate and graduate students struggle with understanding how to successfully navigate their job search and differentiate themselves from other candidates. I also found that, to compound matters, most students didn't relate to the majority of job search books already on the market.

Armed with this information, I realized I had to find a way to help students consider their job searches in a different context, something with which everyone could relate. The metaphor of dating and relationships is perfect! In both cases, you need to figure out what you're looking for, make a great first impression, and convince the other person that you're better than the competition. Moreover, just as not all dates lead to relationships, not all interviews lead to jobs.

Like other undergraduate and graduate students I've counseled, you, too, will find that even the most difficult career-related issues can be broken down and resolved using the simple comparisons and strategies detailed in this book. Each part focuses on a different stage of a relationship's progression—from initial attraction to getting serious. I am convinced that, with the help of the advice and proven suggestions contained in this book, you'll find career success.

Acknowledgments

To say that this book would not have been possible without the help, feedback, and support of others would be an understatement. I would like to thank Susan Pearsall for editing, and helping me to structure, what would become *Courting Your Career.* Thanks also to Melanie Sinche for introducing me to Susan and for always being willing to review my latest revisions. Much appreciation goes to Marcia Harris for helping me navigate the publishing process and for introducing me to Howard Figler, whose contributions to this book have been immeasurable. Thanks to Jonathan Minori (www.minoflow.com) and Andrew Baugh for creating my Web site and to artist extraordinaire Kevin Dixon (ultrakevin@hotmail.com) for creating the cool cartoons in the book.

A huge debt of gratitude to the Carolina undergraduates and MBAs who participated in focus groups to help refine the book into what it is today. Thanks also to Lori Cates Hand and the team at JIST Publishing for believing in this project and for helping to make it a success.

I can't forget about my coworkers and colleagues who've had to endure more than their fair share of hearing about the book but yet still were always willing to lend their support: Susan Amey and the entire Career Management Center team (both past and present), Allison Adams, Lynn Setzer, and Heidi Shultz.

To all the people who contributed quotes for the book (and whose names have been changed to keep me from being sued), many thanks for your insights.

To the Burrito Bunker crew for keeping me nourished along the way. And to Arthur, a fellow patron, who helped me articulate the essence of this book.

Last, but definitely not least, I would like to thank my friends and family for all of their support.

Contents

Chapter 4: Physical Attraction: Creating Eye-Catching Resumes and Cover Letters 51

Chapter 5: Finding Mr. or Ms. Right: Job Search Resources 77

Chapter 6: What Are You Going to Wear?: Dressing for Interview Success 97

Chapter 7: Getting Ready: Interview Prep 105

Chapter 9: Getting Serious: Accepting, Negotiating, and Declining Job Offers 145

Chapter 10: You've Made Your Match: Job Search Lessons Learned 163

Foreword

I've learned a thing or two about career success and relationships in my life.

After attending Yale College and Harvard Business School, I went on to be the youngest person tapped for partner at Deloitte Consulting and the youngest chief marketing officer in the Fortune 500 upon joining Starwood Hotels by age 32. And when people asked me for my biggest secret to success, I knew the answer: building great relationships.

You see, I started at the bottom, born the son of a cleaning lady and an oft-unemployed steelworker. But through the mutually beneficial, generous relationships I (and, when I was very young, my father) cultivated, I was able to rise above my starting station in life. Giving my time and energy to help others be more successful, asking them for help when I needed it, and accepting generosity when it was offered...all that came to me as naturally as breathing. I even wrote a book—*Never Eat Alone*—about building relationships for career success that is now an international bestseller.

That said, I must admit that when I first saw this book's premise, I was a little worried because I'm not nearly as good at dating as I am at the business variety of meeting people. It's just as hard for me as it is for everyone else. Well, if you had a similar concern, I'm here to tell you there's nothing to fear.

In *Courting Your Career*, Shawn Graham isn't saying you have to be great at dating to find a great job. He simply presents the analogy of finding a significant other so that you'll understand better than ever how to go about landing your next job or internship. By drawing parallels to the often challenging and even hilarious situations we've all experienced when looking for Mr. or Ms. Right, Shawn has absolutely demystified the process of taking that next step in your career.

If you pay attention to the advice Shawn shares from his extensive experience counseling countless undergraduate and graduate students, I know that when you finish reading this book, you'll have a firm grasp of the knowledge, skills, and resources you will need to land a great job or internship. Then who knows...maybe your job-hunting acumen will help you find your soulmate.

Keith Ferrazzi

Author, *Never Eat Alone: And Other Secrets to Success, One Relationship at a Time*
www.nevereatalone.com

Chapter 1

What's Your Type?: Identifying Your Interests and Exploring Your Career Options

"They [job searches and dating] both hurt at times because they both involve trying to be the best you can be, getting your hopes up, and either getting that ecstasy of acceptance or that sadness of rejection."

—Hunter, job seeker

What's your type? Tall, dark, and handsome? Short, pale, and ugly? You've probably tried to answer that question a thousand times when it comes to dating. Some people think they know what they're looking for in a potential partner, whereas others rely on astrological signs. Or, if they're one of the roughly 60 percent of men and women responding to a poll conducted by *Cosmopolitan* magazine, they believe in love at first sight.[1]

---

1. "Passion Poll: Do You Believe in Love at First Sight?" *Cosmopolitan.* http://ivillage.divinems.com/servlet/CommonOpinion?cmd=results&id=2/18/126. Accessed 2 March 2004.

At face value, determining "your type" sounds like a simple concept, but is it really? Without understanding yourself first, finding your perfect match is going to be next to impossible. Unfortunately, a lack of self-awareness is evident not only in the world of dating, but also during the job search, when it occurs all too often. As a result, to avoid the uncertainty associated with change, we often seek out a new relationship that is similar to the one we just left, regardless of whether we were happy there. Don't jump from one bad relationship to another. It's time to break the cycle!

One question I often asked undergraduate and graduate students when they came in for career advice is what they wanted to do when they graduated. "I have no idea" or "I just want a job in New York" were two common responses. I followed up by asking them their majors and why they chose those areas of study. We also talked about classes they particularly liked to see if there was any correlation to their college major. By discussing their choices, I was helping them to connect the dots between decisions that might have appeared unrelated. If you decide to look for a job in New York to be closer to family or a boyfriend or girlfriend, that's great. You've put some thought into your decision and added some focus to your search. On the other hand, saying "I don't care what kind of job I take as long as it pays the bills" is almost like saying "I just want someone with teeth" when asked what you're looking for in a mate.

Self-awareness is critical to an effective job search because it enables you to determine what you want from your next opportunity. When you know what you're looking for, you can target careers or organizations that fit your wants and needs. This chapter focuses on the importance of self-awareness in your job search and also provides advice on gathering career information and ways to prioritize what's most important to you when looking for a great job.

Finding Yourself: Career Research

The first step in figuring out what you're looking for in a future mate is to look back at past relationships. Say, for example, you've recently broken up with someone. Why did things end? Was he or she cheating on you? Did you outgrow each other? Was the timing just wrong? Were you to blame for the breakup? Because most of us aren't psychic and can't predict the future, learning from the past is the best way to avoid repeating mistakes and to gain a better sense of what you want and expect from your next relationship. The same holds true for your job search. Start out by asking yourself questions about positions you've previously held including the following:

> *Self-awareness is of the utmost importance.... Being confident and knowing who you are not only allows you to best know what you're looking for, but it is also an appealing quality—both to potential dating partners and potential employers.*
>
> —Deena, teacher

- What did you like? Your boss's management style? Positive relationships with your coworkers? Daily tasks? Opportunities for advancement?

- What didn't you like? Your boss? Your coworkers? Daily tasks? A lack of adequate training?

Based on your responses to these questions, what would you want your new job to look like?

Who *Isn't* Your Type: Ruling Out What You Don't Want to Do

When you're not sure what you want to do, your job search can seem overwhelming. To get the ball rolling, another strategy is to think about what you *don't* want to do—the dating version of "What turns me on? What turns me off?" By ruling out things you don't like first, you'll be able to target things you do like.

As you start to eliminate different jobs, consider multiple sources of information before making any final decisions. That way, you'll avoid excluding a certain job based on bad advice or one person's opinion.

The key to these exercises is you. Be honest with yourself. Finding the right career requires you to know yourself inside and out. In a good situation, how did you feel, and why was it good for you? In a bad situation, what did you do to try to improve things?

I once counseled a client about to graduate from college who had spent so much time on her studies, she hadn't taken time to think about what kind of job she wanted to pursue after graduation. With only a few months before she finished school, she didn't know where to begin and, in a panic, thought she might end up having to settle for the first job that came along, regardless of whether she was interested in it. By utilizing the Self-Directed Search (SDS; discussed in the appendix) and working with other career resources to research different occupations, she was able to identify and land a job she enjoyed. During her job search, she also learned a valuable lesson: You don't have to marry your first date just because you're afraid no one else will ever come along.

Getting to Know Yourself

Make a list of jobs you think you might like. Then consider the reasons you're interested in them. As you gather more and more information about yourself, you'll eventually reach a deeper understanding of what you're looking for—both personally and professionally. During your job search, you can use this insight to target employers and positions that fit your personality and skills. When you consider relationships, you can also take advantage of your increased self-awareness to determine whether you're compatible with someone. In both cases, self-awareness is a lifelong process, and it will continue to play an important role in your ability to locate jobs and develop personal relationships that are right for you in the future.

Five Ways to Increase Your Self-Awareness

1. Visit your campus career center or local library.
   - Utilize self-assessment resources.
   - Research careers.
2. Talk to classmates, professors, and family.
3. Rule something out.
4. "Shadow" people in jobs of interest.
5. Work as an intern or volunteer or complete a practicum project.

A number of self-awareness resources are available to help you sort things out. Some are career-related, whereas others focus mainly on your personality and interests. I know what you're thinking. "A friend of mine took one of those tests once, and it told him he was going to be a funeral director." Somehow, it's like we've all had that friend. Urban legend or not, don't let that stop you from taking them. Keep in mind that these resources are designed to serve only as guides, not to tell you exactly which job you should choose.

Best case, you uncover a career area or job you've never thought about before, or the test results confirm something you already know. Worst case, the test results suggest a job or career area that doesn't interest you, and you're out a few hours of your time (or we end up with a major surplus of funeral directors). Regardless of whether you agree or disagree with the results, take some time to think what's behind them. Don't get caught up in job titles or career areas. Instead, look at the underlying details. If your results suggest you'd make a great funeral director, maybe the real reason is that you'd like to work with people in a helping profession. If dealing with the dearly departed isn't your cup of tea, think about what other jobs might be out there.

The tests mentioned previously create a snapshot of your personality, interests, skills, and ways of communicating with others, all of which are essential components of self-knowledge.

If you are currently enrolled in a college or university, visit the career center on campus to see which resources are available to assist you in your career decision-making process. If the center has a career library, spend some time reading different self-assessment books and checking out related Web sites. Be sure to meet with one of the counselors there and get some assistance right from the start.

Much like dating sites such as eHarmony use systems to match your compatibility with other singles, self-assessment resources might help you match your compatibility with specific jobs and careers. There are a ton to choose from, but we'll focus on two of my favorites. A detailed breakdown of some of the other popular ones is included in the appendix.

- **Campbell Interest and Skills Survey (CISS):** Created by Dr. David Campbell, this survey measures self-reported vocational interests and skills. In addition to measuring an individual's attraction to specific occupations, this resource goes beyond other traditional inventories by measuring a person's confidence when performing various occupational activities. Because it examines interests and personal confidence, this survey is more comprehensive than an interest survey alone. The CISS focuses on careers that require a postsecondary education and is used mainly by individuals who are college-bound or those who have a college degree. Completion time: approximately 25 minutes.

- **Strong Interest Inventory (Strong):** Based on the concept that individuals are more productive and satisfied when they work in jobs or at tasks they find interesting, the Strong can be used to assist you with a number of issues, such as making career decisions, determining a proper work-life balance, and choosing appropriate training and education. Completion time: approximately 25 minutes.

If you're in college, check with your campus career center for cost and availability of these self-assessment resources. If you don't have access to a college or university career center, you can find these self-assessment resources using your favorite Internet search engine. For starters, check out ReadyMinds at www.readyminds.com. This resource offers distance career-counseling programs for all levels of work experience, from student to experienced career changer.

You can also check the Yellow Pages or YellowPages.com for counselors or psychologists who offer career counseling in your area. Most career counselors will be familiar with personality and skills inventories and can assist you in analyzing the results.

Researching Careers and Industries

Want information that might help you land a date? Read articles in *Maxim* or *Cosmopolitan*. Want information that will help you land a job? Read the *Wall Street Journal*, industry publications, related magazines, and company Web sites.

Industry Resources

To better understand specific industries and therefore maximize your job search success, take time to familiarize yourself with resources that focus on careers and industries in which you are interested. The more you present yourself like an insider, the more likely you'll be one. See the list of sample industry publications in the sidebar on this page to help you get started. You can read the print editions of these publications or access them online.

Sample Industry Publications

- *Advertising Age*
- *Barron's*
- *Brandweek*
- *Business Week*
- *Consulting Magazine*
- *The Ecologist*
- *The Economist*
- *Entrepreneur*
- *Forbes*
- *Fortune*
- *HR Magazine*

- *Industry Week* (manufacturing)
- *Institutional Investor*
- *Investor's Business Daily*
- *Journal of Accountancy*
- *Journal of Management Consulting*
- *Kiplinger's*
- *Money*
- *National Real Estate Investor*
- *Red Herring*
- *Roll Call* (Congressional news)
- *Sales and Marketing Management*

When you first start to gather career information, the sheer quantity of it and the variety of sources and resources might seem overwhelming, but don't get discouraged. Instead, think of your search like looking for a new boyfriend or girlfriend. During the first few weeks, you might not know where to begin. As overwhelming as that can seem, you'll ultimately start to narrow your search to those people you are really attracted to and connect with. The same holds true with your job search. Although exploring all your options takes more work, you'll almost always be happier in the end because you will have made an informed decision based on the best available information.

Always Have a Backup

Just as you probably kept e-mails and notes from someone you were dating when you were in junior high, you should also keep a hard copy of any information you find helpful during your job search. This includes information about the companies you're applying to and descriptions of the positions you're applying for. Now is the time to be organized. Keep a file folder of newspaper clippings, printouts of materials you found on the Web, brochures you collect at career fairs, and so on. Web sites change on a daily basis, and newspapers and books may not always be readily available. If you always have a hard copy in your possession, you won't have to worry about locating important job information when you need it most—such as the job description the night before you interview for a job.

Career Resources

Knowing and understanding what you're looking for in a relationship or a job is critical. After all, if you don't know what you want, you won't know when you find it. In addition to using the resources mentioned in the preceding section, you can gather information about possible careers in a number of other ways.

The *Occupational Information Network* (O*NET™), available at online.onetcenter.org/, is a comprehensive database of worker competencies, job requirements, resources, and other information offered by the U.S. Department of Labor. With O*NET, you can search for information on specific occupations, such as occupations that match your skill sets or experience. Say you're interested in working as a sales manager, but you're not sure what that job would involve. Search the database for "sales manager." For each position, you'll find a general overview, associated tasks, required knowledge, skills, abilities, and other pertinent information. Read each position report to determine whether the job is something you'd consider and conduct additional research on those you find interesting.

The U.S. Department of Labor also publishes the *Occupational Outlook Handbook* at www.bls.gov/oco/. Similar to O*NET, this resource enables you to learn about different occupations, but it also provides valuable information about the job outlook for each occupation. Although no one can predict the future, you should definitely take into consideration the anticipated demand for workers to fill particular jobs over the next few years. You can access both of these resources free of charge 24 hours a day online.

In addition to O*NET and the *Occupational Outlook Handbook,* other popular career resources are available online. Check the appendix for a complete list, including a description of each site.

A number of career exploration resources are also available at your local public library. There, you will find helpful tools that include industry journals and guides that provide detailed information about careers in a number of industries.

Most public libraries subscribe to fee-based databases such as ABI/Inform (Proquest), Business Source (Ebsco), and Infotrac (Gale). These databases provide access to thousands of articles from newspapers, magazines, and other periodicals. They can be a great source for locating company and industry information.

At a public library, you can also gather real-time information on various industries and the economy by browsing hard-copy periodicals such as the *Wall Street Journal* and the *New York Times*. While you're there, be sure to ask a reference librarian for recommendations on other excellent resources for company and industry research.

For a list of public libraries in your area, visit PublicLibraries.com at www.publiclibraries.com. In addition, many academic libraries, particularly at public colleges and universities, are open to local residents.

Flirting: Informational Interviews/Career Shadowing

Like flirting with someone you'd like to get to know better before asking that person out on a date, informational interviews and career shadowing offer you a chance to learn about the world of employment before you decide on a career. As such, it's important that you do quite a bit of research before reaching out to possible contacts. After all, you're going to be contacting people and asking them to take time to speak with you about their jobs during an informational interview or allow you to shadow, or follow them around, on the job. You need to have a firm grasp on what you want to do so that you can ask educated questions. You wouldn't want to miss out on a great opportunity to learn from someone firsthand about his or her job by wasting that time on basic questions. Keep in mind that you might not be able to shadow people working in professions that require a high level of client confidentiality. For example, you wouldn't be able to shadow a psychologist.

Ice Breakers: Informational Interview Questions

If you're anything like me, you've probably planned—maybe even rehearsed—several possible conversation starters in front of the mirror before going on a first date. Likewise, when you prepare for an informational interview, it's a good idea to write a list of questions you want to ask ahead of time. That way, you're less likely to stumble your way through that first sometimes awkward introduction. If someone is willing to spend time talking with you, it's important not to waste that opportunity. Spend some time beforehand developing well-thought-out questions. That way, you'll be able to get answers to questions you might not have thought of asking.

Questions you might want to ask include the following:

- How did you get into this field?
- Tell me about your role. What kinds of projects do you work on?
- What do you enjoy most about your job? What do you enjoy least?
- What skills and abilities are critical for success for someone in your position?
- What subject areas would you recommend I focus on in college if I'm interested in this career field?
- What publications/Web sites do you read to stay current in your field?
- Why did you choose this field?
- What are the biggest challenges facing your industry?
- If you were about to graduate from college, how would you go about getting into this field?
- Can you recommend other people in your line of work I might be able to speak with?

Six Effective Ways to Learn About Possible Careers

1. Check print resources.
2. Use the Internet.
3. Schedule informational interviews.
4. Consult friends, family, and professors.
5. Attend career fairs.
6. Investigate internships.

During your conversation, you can also describe what you want to do and ask the person you're meeting with whether he or she knows of a job in the field that matches what you hope to do. You might find an occupation you weren't aware of that fits your interests and abilities better than your previous career interest.

Managing Expectations

When you contact people in search of career information, be clear from the start about what you hope to gain from the interaction. (CAUTION: This strategy will not work with potential dates. In the dating world, this interaction amounts to something like, "Hi there, my name is Carl. I would like to take you on a date, eventually get married, and have 2.5 children. What's your name?") When you're trying to gather information about a certain career such as which skills are necessary or what the career path typically looks like, let your contact person know what you are looking for and keep your conversation focused on these issues. Take a look at a sample cold-calling script for contacting someone to schedule an informational interview.

Sample Script: Calling to Schedule an Informational Interview

You: Good morning [insert his or her name]. My name is [insert your name] and I am a recent graduate of Purdue University with a bachelor's degree in business administration. I am calling because I am interested in pursuing a career in business development. I would like to schedule 15 to 20 minutes to talk to you about your role with [insert company name]. In particular, I'm looking for information about similar career paths and felt that you might be able to steer me in the right direction.

(continued)

(continued)

Roadblock

Interviewee: "Sorry, I'm really busy, so I'm going to have to pass."

Possible Response

You: "If now is not a good time, perhaps we can schedule something in a few weeks if that works better for you."

OR

You: "I'm sorry to hear that. Do you happen to know of anyone else I can speak to?"

THE BAIT AND SWITCH

Describe myself? Well, I'm 5' 4", with hazel eyes and long auburn hair. I like long walks in the park....

Figure 1.1: The bait and switch.

The least effective strategy is the old "bait and switch" technique, where you bait people to agree to talk to you for informational purposes and then switch to asking them instead about jobs with their company. In the world of dating, this is known as the "let's be friends" approach, where a person whose sole interest is a romantic relationship masks his or her intentions in friendship. I'm sure you've seen it happen. Finding out that your "friend" actually had no interest in a platonic relationship can be really awkward. However, if you're meeting with someone to gather information, and he or she brings up the topic of possible jobs or internships, then all bets are off. In that case, you have every right to express your interest and ask questions about possible openings.

Taking Notes

As you conduct informational interviews and shadow different people, make sure you take detailed notes. After all, the information you gather during these interactions is going to help you when you're deciding on what jobs to pursue. Your notes will also help you personalize your thank-you letters and follow-up e-mails (see chapter 8 for more on these). Keep track of conversations, the names of people you've met, their positions, where they went to school, what their hobbies are, and any other information you think might come in handy. Make sure you remember how to pronounce their names in case you end up meeting with them again. If you're worried about getting the pronunciation right, spell out the name phonetically.

Finding People for Informational Interviews

To locate people to approach about possible informational interviews or career-shadowing experiences, check with your campus career office for available resources and speak with family, friends, and classmates. For others, check your college alumni database; talk with friends, family, and current or former coworkers; or identify and contact someone currently working in a position similar to the one you're interested in. We'll talk more about how to reach out to people during your job search in chapter 3.

Casual Dating: Internships, Practicum Projects, and Volunteer Work

Like casual dating, internships, practicum projects, and volunteer work offer you and the company an opportunity to get to know each other better without being locked into a long-term commitment. They're a great way to gain valuable work experience you can put on your resume and can also help you choose your career path.

Why Internships Matter

One of the most important benefits of an internship is gathering information on a specific job that will assist you in making career decisions. As you work, you may find the experience has reaffirmed your interest in a certain career; or, on the other hand, you may just be interested in getting the hell out of there. Because these options are short term in nature (eight to ten weeks), you don't have to worry about making a long-term commitment as you learn about different career fields. However, you still need to make sure that you put your best foot forward by delivering high-quality work.

Intern Heartbreak

Speaking of wanting to get the hell out of there, I once counseled an undergrad who accepted a summer internship with a medium-sized organization that had never hired an intern before. Over the course of the summer, the student received almost no training, had minimal supervision, and ended up spending most of his time watching television while waiting for someone to give him a project to work on.

By the time his internship ended, he had nothing to add to his resume in the way of practical work experience. The only thing he accomplished that summer was developing an addiction to daytime talk shows. To keep this from happening, he could have paid closer attention to details during the interviews to find out what he was going to be responsible for and whom he'd be working with. Conversely, he could have also shown initiative by working on some projects on his own and then sharing the results with his boss.

Internships, practicum projects, and volunteer work can also provide an opportunity for you to gain practical, hands-on experience. This experience can complement your academic studies while at the same time providing you with transferable skills you'll later use on the job. Employers want to see that you're more than book smart. They want to know whether you can apply what you've learned in the classroom to real-world situations and problems. Internships, practicum projects, and volunteer work all offer opportunities for you to showcase your talents.

If you play your cards right and depending on the organization, there's often a chance the internship could lead to long-term romance—a full-time position. Employers consistently rate their internship program as the best method of hiring college and graduate students, and for good reason. Internships are a talent pipeline for companies and lower the costs of employee turnover. Plus, interns already know most of the ins and outs of the company, so they're better able to hit the ground running as full-time employees. According to a survey published by the National Association of Colleges and

Employers, approximately 76 percent of employers report higher retention among college graduates who interned or completed cooperative-education assignments with their company versus those who didn't.[2]

Developing professional contacts can obviously be another significant benefit of participating in an internship, especially people you can list as references during your job search.

Choosing an Internship

As you consider different options for gaining experience while you're in school, make sure you have a clear understanding of what your responsibilities would be at each position and the level of training you would receive. If a job description is not available, see whether the company would be willing to work with you to create one. It doesn't have to be anything formal, just five or six key things you hope to accomplish by the end of the experience. That way, if you get off track, you can reference the work plan during your next meeting with your supervisor. Unfortunately, not everyone thinks to talk about job content before accepting internships or volunteer positions.

When evaluating different internships, try to get a feel for the type of people who'll be supervising you before you make your final decision. Do they seem enthusiastic at the prospect of mentoring you? Do they have enough time to take someone under their wing? Are they looking forward to getting some help on some specific projects? And after you accept a position, make the best of it. If you find that you want additional responsibilities after you start, don't be afraid to ask for them. Volunteering to take on additional projects or assignments not only shows your supervisor that you have drive and initiative, but also helps you get the most out of your experience. Waiting until the end of your internship before you speak up doesn't help you or the organization you are interning with.

TIP: Like casually dating someone, internships, practicum projects, and volunteer work offer you and the company an opportunity to get to know each other better without being locked into a long-term commitment.

---

2. National Association of Colleges and Employers. "2005 Experiential Education Survey." http://naceweb.org/press/display.asp?year=&prid=220. Accessed 24 September 2005.

Seek out opportunities that provide the best chance for you to develop your skills while also gaining valuable work experience. Don't feel as though you need to settle for something that focuses entirely on secretarial work (unless you are an aspiring secretary) or on work that's not related to the career you plan to pursue. Likewise, don't be afraid to roll up your sleeves. Pitching in around the office shows your employer that you have a strong work ethic and that you're willing to do what it takes to get the job done. This is especially true if you're interested in working for a smaller company. In some cases, such companies may lack administrative support and therefore need to rely on all team members to pitch in around the office.

Try not to select a position solely based on pay (the equivalent of dating someone solely based on looks). Some of the best opportunities can come from unpaid or low-paying internships or from working as a volunteer. When you look back on your career, chances are you're not going to remember how much money you made over the summer. Finding a position that gives you the skills and experience to launch your career after graduation is far more important than a few thousand dollars. If you're planning on accepting an unpaid internship, it may be possible for you to receive academic credit or community service hours. Check with your college or university career office or academic department for details.

Use Your Internship to Network

Networking can be a critical step in locating a job, so you'll need to develop a strong base of contacts. During your internship, take time to meet people within the organization. Attend social events sponsored by your employer, grab lunch with members of your team, and be sure to reach out to other interns.

In addition to networking with people internally, contact alumni working at other companies of interest in the area. Getting to know people during your internship not only helps your chances of getting an offer, but can also help you hedge your risk if you don't get an offer from your intern employer by expanding your list of contacts outside the company.

Before you actually start doing it, "networking" may sound as potentially painful and terrifying as asking a stranger out for a date. However, it's so important to your career search that we'll discuss it in depth in chapter 3.

Internships, by their nature, come at a time in your life when you have the least insider knowledge. The decisions you make about the internships you choose can have a huge impact on the success of your full-time job search. Therefore, it's a good idea to get some professional advice before you select an internship. Consult with a helpful counselor or professor, who should be able to help you read the fine print and predict whether a given internship will truly be beneficial to your career plans. He or she also might be familiar with internship programs that place you in cities throughout the United States and abroad.

TIP: Most college career centers maintain a database of internship and volunteer openings, so be sure to check with them before starting your search. There are also a number of great Web sites (see the appendix for a list).

You've thought about what you're looking for in a career and you've gathered information on different careers. It's now time prioritize the things you want most from your dream job. You've come a long way from just wanting someone with teeth, haven't you?

Does Size Really Matter? Prioritizing Your Career Interests

Is someone's weight or looks really what's most important to you, or are you more interested in someone with a great personality who is fun to be around? You've been gathering information on different career options, and now it's time to start prioritizing.

> *Without being aware of what is important to you, the reason for taking a job or continuing a relationship may be unclear; thus in time you may find yourself unhappy with your job choice or relationship.*
>
> —Blake, job seeker

Making Your Wish List

Although no single method works best when you're ranking your career interests, making a list of everything you're looking for in a career—a "wish list"—can be very effective. Use the sample Career Wish List in this section to outline your likes and dislikes for each career area. These can include job-related tasks, potential coworkers, geographic location, and practical concerns such as commute time.

When you have this list, imagine that you have to give up three things to land your dream job. What would that second list look like?

Would size of the company or money be at the top of the list? How about job content? Will you be more likely to feel bored or energized in each of the types of jobs you're considering? Then imagine being all set to start the new job and finding out the position will be in an area where you just don't want to live. Will your list change yet again? Eventually, you'll boil it down to a few critical traits.

At the beginning of this exercise of narrowing down job targets, some people would say money is a major factor in deciding on a particular job or career field. This priority is much like in the world of dating, where people often focus primarily on physical appearance when trying to locate that special someone. In the beginning, a hot body or pretty face might be what is most important to you, but would these factors be as important if the person you're dating was a major pain in the neck or a total idiot? A good buddy of mine dated just such a girl. She was very attractive, but I swear I've talked to walls that had better personalities. Needless to say, her looks went only so far—as did their relationship, which soon ended. Similarly, you could find a job that would pay you a ton of money and that might be awesome for a little while, but if you hate your job, how long are you going to stick around?

After you've finalized your list, take a look at what you value most from a possible career and remember that your priorities will change over time. At one point, I was absolutely unwilling to leave Pennsylvania for any job opportunities. I often reminisce with one of my former supervisors about this point in my life. He was encouraging me to widen my search to opportunities outside Pennsylvania, and I can remember my response to this day: "Nope, nope, nope, never, nope, nope." Yet today, I've been living in North Carolina for more than six years and couldn't be happier about my personal life or my career.

Career Wish List

Career area: _____

Likes: _____

_____

_____

_____

Dislikes: _____

_____

_____

_____

Career area: _____

Likes: _____

_____

_____

_____

Dislikes: _____

_____

_____

_____

Finding a career that meets every one of your needs and expectations is difficult, but don't let that dissuade you from creating a wish list before you really start looking. As I said earlier, it's very important to aim high, to avoid seeking "a spouse or partner with teeth" or a "job that pays." But the reverse is true, too. Some items on your wish list won't be as important to you in the long run. If you find a terrific job that lacks opportunities for you to express your creative side and that is something important to you, there may be a way to address this need by asking to take on a new project or through a hobby or some other avenue. You also might be looking for a job that will give you the skills to transition to another line of work a few years down the road. By spending time figuring out what you value most from a job, you'll be better able to find something you truly enjoy instead of just settling on something sexy that may or may not have any substance.

How Much Does Money Matter?

Deloitte Consulting conducted a poll on its Web site asking visitors to indicate their "number one" career priority.[3] Participants could vote for money, security, promotions, learning, coworkers, mentors, or corporate culture. Learning came in first, with approximately 43 percent of the vote. Money came in a distant second, with just over 20 percent of the vote. We also know from a number of other studies that money isn't always the prime factor when it comes to on-the-job happiness. You may even find that to earn the kind of money you think you want, you'll have to work a lot harder than you're actually willing to work.

Smaller Companies Versus Larger Companies

Before we move on, let's take a quick look at some positives and negatives of working for smaller companies and how those factors compare to working for larger companies. Your decision to work for a smaller company or a larger company will depend on what you hope to gain. Working for a well-known company can be great, but if all you're doing is making copies, you won't have anything to put on your resume. Likewise, working for a smaller company won't do you any good if you spend most of your time twiddling your thumbs. In most cases, you'll find opportunities that land somewhere in the middle—a well-known company that allows you to work on meaningful projects.

Smaller Companies	Larger Companies
+ Flexibility to define your job or internship	+ Structured recruiting program with clearly defined jobs and internships and more opportunities for formal, internal training
+ Exposure to upper management	+ Amount of work
+ Level of responsibility on projects	+ Broad exposure to managers/management
+ Opportunity to strike it rich or move up the ladder more quickly if the company is growing incredibly fast	+ Company name recognition
– Lack of brand	+ Higher compensation
– Lack of structured orientation or training	– Access to upper management could be limited
– Compensation could be lower than that at a larger company	– Not as much input in defining your job or internship as with smaller companies

3. "Poll: My Number One Career Priority Is." Deloitte Consulting. http://careers.deloitte.com/poll_results.aspx?PollID=30. Accessed 1 November 2003.

Chapter 2

Playing the Field: Developing Your Job Search Plan

Because arranged marriages aren't as common as they used to be, most of us have to play the field to find that special someone. And when we do, we're usually first drawn to certain people based on physical attraction or personality, or in a perfect world some combination of both. Although narrowing your focus can have its benefits, when you first start out looking for that special someone, it's usually a good idea to cast a wide net if you want to maximize your opportunities for romance. Doing so gives you a chance to consider people you might not otherwise be attracted to. The same holds true when looking for jobs. Narrowing your initial search to an advertising position with a company with 5 to 75 employees located in northern Montana could significantly limit your chances of finding a job.

However, in your job search, unlike the world of dating, where strategies to find that special someone occur mostly on a subconscious level, at some point you will need to develop a more concrete career strategy than just playing the field. If you haven't developed (or even heard of) a job search strategy before, you're not alone. According to a survey conducted by the career management organization Bernard Haldane Associates, only 9 percent of 200 adult respondents indicated that they planned job searches.[1]

One job seeker I counseled had decided to focus his search on a very specific geographic area by applying only for positions located a short distance from his hometown. For some, this strategy can be very effective. In this case, however, the young man mentioned that he wasn't having much luck, so we discussed the possibility of broadening his search. Over the next few weeks, he was able to uncover a number of positions to apply for, and he eventually ended up accepting a truly rewarding opportunity in another state. Similar to my job search situation mentioned in chapter 1, by being flexible in his search, this man was able to find a job he thoroughly enjoyed.

Keeping in mind the previous discussion about the drawbacks of dating someone just because that person is good-looking, during your job search it's important to look beyond the superficial characteristics of potential employers, such as the image created by their marketing teams. Instead, focus on the people at the company and the responsibilities of the job they're advertising. Whom do you know who works or has worked at that company? Is he or she the kind of person you could work with? A brand-new office building filled with expensive furniture is nice, but if you can't stand working there, having nice surroundings won't make you happy.

Beyond "Someone with Teeth": Determining Your Job Search Priorities

Determining your priorities is the first step toward formulating a job search strategy. You'll need to consider your answers to questions such as the following:

---

1. Bernard Haldane Associates. "Career Survey." www.haldane.com/careers/survey.htm. Accessed 3 March 2004.

- What is your time frame? Do you need to find a job in a week? A month? Six months?

- Are you looking for jobs that offer a lot of autonomy?

- How important is job content?

- Would you like to work for a small company, a not-for-profit, or a large corporation?

- Do you want to focus on companies in a certain geographic region?

- Would you like to direct, manage, or supervise the activities of others?

- Are you looking for jobs that offer opportunities for rapid advancement?

- How important is money? What salary range are you willing to consider?

- Would you like to work with a team or by yourself?

- Are you willing to travel? If so, how much?

- Would you like a job in which your duties changed frequently, or would you prefer routine work?

By enabling you to focus your efforts on organizations you are truly interested in, answering these questions before you start looking at companies will save you a lot of work in the long run. In contrast, I've counseled a lot of clients who have adopted an "I'll take anything and everything" approach to their job search; they simply applied to a large number of organizations at the same time. Although this strategy can work, the success rate is limited because you're focusing more on application quantity versus quality. If you are submitting cover letters to each organization, it's very difficult to give them the personal touch necessary to catch the recruiter's attention. Looking at the shotgun approach another way, think about your likely success rate of finding a date if you walked into a bar and introduced yourself to everyone in sight. You'd probably meet a lot of people, but you'd have a difficult time developing any meaningful relationships.

Don't confuse casting a wide net with the shotgun approach. When you cast a wide net, you're hedging your risk by focusing on a manageable number of opportunities. With the shotgun approach, you're applying to anything and everything that comes your way (not manageable). As a result, you don't have time to do things right. Instead, you end up cranking out generic e-mails, cover letters, and resumes, thus diminishing your chances of landing a great job.

I'm Going to Find a Partner Before Summer: Setting Job Search Goals

Without standards, you might end up settling for the first person who gives you the time of day, just so you can be in a relationship. Then you'll wake up one morning wondering how you could have ever been attracted to the mean, moody, controlling person you've been dating, let alone living with, for the past six months. The same holds true during your job search. Having standards and setting goals will enable you to measure your successes and help you to stay organized and on task for the duration of your search.

Characteristics of Effective Goals

Effective goals contain five key characteristics, commonly referred to by the acronym *S.M.A.R.T.*, which stands for

- **Specific:** When you're trying to reach a goal, the more clearly defined it can be, the greater the likelihood that you will achieve a meaningful goal. Being specific doesn't mean "I'm going to start looking for a job." Rather, it means "I'm going to e-mail three networking contacts this week."

- **Measurable:** To determine whether you're getting closer to achieving your goal, you have to be able to measure your progress. For example, did you e-mail three networking contacts this week?

- **Attainable:** To be effective, your goals should be challenging but also realistic. Setting a goal that's impossible to reach is meaningless (for example, hoping to date Paris Hilton or Jake Gyllenhaal, or to land a VP role at Microsoft straight out of college).

- **Relevant:** Your goals should reinforce your long-term objective. Let's say your ultimate goal is to find an internship with a biotechnology company. Relevant goals are the steps you can take along the way that might help you land that internship. An example might be meeting with people who are currently working in the field. In this case, setting a goal to network with five people each week is relevant only if it helps you attain your goal.

- **Timely:** Establish a time frame and stick to it. This will give you a sense of urgency and an ending point to strive for. Set deadlines for both short- and longer-term goals. A timely goal might be "I will secure a marketing position within the next three months."

Be Proactive

The earlier you start researching careers and participating in internships, the better your chances of choosing a major and courses that match your career area of interest. By completing multiple internships, you'll gain skills and experience that will significantly increase your chance of finding the job you want after graduation. As much as you might love a certain major or class, that doesn't mean you'll love a particular job or career related to it. Internships give you a chance to apply what you've learned in the classroom to a real-world setting.

Whether you're a college student looking for a job or internship, or you are looking for your third or fourth job, treat your search like it's a class. Block off some time for networking, searching for positions, and so on (see figure 2.1). Although there is no exact formula, you might want to consider allocating your time based on the documented effectiveness of each job search method. For example, employment surveys consistently rank networking as the best source for a new job, with 60 to 70 percent of respondents reporting they found their position through networking and the remaining 30 to 40 percent coming from search firms, advertisements, the Internet, and direct resume mailings. As your search progresses, you may find that you're having more success with the Internet or advertisements than you are with networking. In that case, it might make sense to reallocate your time accordingly.

Sunday	Monday	Tuesday	Wednesday	Thursday	Friday	Saturday
1	2 Conduct career research	3	4	5	6	7
8	9	10	11	12	13	14
15	16 Develop networking contacts	17	18	19	20	21
22	23	24	25	26	27	28
29	30	31				

Figure 2.1: A sample job search time-allocation plan.

How Long Will All of This Take?

The length of a typical full-time job search varies, but the average search can last anywhere from one to six months. Looking at statistics from the U.S. Bureau of Labor Statistics over the past 10 years, the average number of weeks people have remained unemployed has ranged anywhere from as low as 12.2 weeks in 2000 to as high as 19.8 weeks in 2004.[2] With that in mind, establish your timeline by determining when you hope to start your next job. If you're currently employed, think about how long you are willing to stay at your present position while you look for a new opportunity. Likewise, if you are currently unemployed, determine how long you can afford to search before you'll need to secure employment under any circumstances.

---

2. "Survey: Labor Force Statistics from the Current Population Survey." U.S. Department of Labor. Bureau of Labor Statistics. http://data.bls.gov/cgi-bin/surveymost. Accessed 23 February 2004.

Based on the total amount of time you have to work with, break your search into manageable parts. Let's say you have two semesters to work with. Here's a sample plan:

1. Take the first two to three weeks to determine what jobs you are interested in and to target organizations that offer such positions.

2. After you've made a list of companies you're most interested in, over the next two to three weeks, utilize existing contacts or develop new networking contacts at companies where you're applying in an effort to get yourself noticed.

3. Next, tailor your resume and cover letter to the type of job you're targeting. For each position, focus on the things you've done in and out of the classroom that you believe will be of most interest to the employer. These things may include projects, work experience, relevant courses, and honors. (I talk more about customizing your resume in chapter 4.)

4. With three months left, continue to build your networking contacts and start to apply for open positions.

You're Not My Type: Narrowing the Focus of Your Job Search

After you've established your job search goals, you should begin to narrow your focus. As a starting point, reference the information you collected when you were researching different jobs and careers. What are you interested in? Where do you want to live? How much money would you like to make? In chapter 1 you evaluated your interests. Now give some thought to where you want to live and how much money you expect to make.

In both jobs and relationships, you try to find someone (something) that you can be happy with day in and day out.,., You look for someone/thing that won't lose charm and appeal after the initial phases and won't leave you bored or feeling lacking. You look for someone/thing that will inspire you, arouse your passion, and make you come alive. No one wants a dud in a relationship or a job.

—Karen, job seeker

Location, Location, Location

When you're communicating with potential employers, location should generally take a backseat to your interest in the organization and the position you're applying for. If you find the right employer and the right position, chances are the location won't be the major factor in whether you accept the position. To look at the situation another way, say you looked for a potential mate purely based on how close to your house that person lived. Intellect, physical attraction, and other traits were all afterthoughts. This would be a poor strategy, and think about the message this sends to the person who is lucky enough to be your date when he or she finds out you really weren't interested in him or her as a person, but rather, you were more interested in the fact that he or she lived a block away.

Also, keep in mind that you're not signing a lifetime contract with the company. If you find a great opportunity with a great company, but it's in a city you're not crazy about, you can always move someplace else in two or three years after you've gained some great experience.

Although location shouldn't necessarily be in your top two or three priorities, it is important for several reasons. After all, if your search is successful, you'll almost certainly end up living near where you work. Even the best job in the world can get old when you don't like your surroundings. To keep this from happening, try to visit the city you might be moving to before accepting your offer. Don't make a decision based on how nice the airport is. Drive around. If you hear random gunfire at two in the afternoon, that's a good indicator you should keep your head down and get back to the airport as fast as you can.

Depending on the industry you're interested in, you may decide to focus your job search on a specific region, especially if a large number of companies in your selected industry are located in a single geographic area. Examples include advertising, arts, banking, marketing, and nonprofits in New York and consulting in Atlanta.

The Book of Lists reference guides are great resources for identifying leading businesses by geographic area. Available in most campus career center libraries, they contain key contact information on companies in more than 60 U.S. markets, including Atlanta, Boston, Dallas, Los Angeles, and Washington, D.C. Chambers of commerce are also great resources for locating companies in specific cities. Some allow access to their online business directory without requiring membership. For a list of state and local chambers of commerce, visit www.2chambers.com.

By narrowing location, you will be able to maximize your efforts by scheduling multiple informational interviews and other networking trips around the same time, saving time and money. One word of caution, though: Focusing solely on geographic regions can limit your ability to uncover some great opportunities in other parts of the country.

Money Isn't Everything

Again, as with location, look at the best possible positions for your skills, abilities, and interests instead of focusing solely on salary. Your parents probably gave you similar advice when you started looking for your first job: As they said, "money isn't everything"—but nonetheless, money will be an important factor to consider when evaluating different jobs.

Even if you're starting at the bottom rung of the career ladder, being upwardly mobile will help keep you feeling satisfied with almost any job you select. Therefore, I highly recommend looking at openings with organizations that offer opportunities for career advancement. In some cases, you can determine whether such opportunities exist with a particular organization based on whether the company promotes from within. Some companies are more inclined to look internally to fill open positions, whereas others like to look outside the organization for a fresh perspective. If you're interested in having a chance to move up the ranks and you have contacts at the company you're looking at, talk to them to see how their firm views opportunities for advancement.

Don't Be a One-Trick Pony: Benefits of a Multi-Tiered Job Search

To limit your risk of not finding a job in the event that the position you really want doesn't come through, you should consider conducting a multitiered job search. In other words, don't put all your eggs in one basket. A multitiered search doesn't mean focusing all your efforts on Plan A and falling back to Plan B or Plan C if things don't work out. Rather, it means conducting searches simultaneously so you can establish networking relationships and apply for positions in each area of interest.

Say, for example, your top choice would be to work in broadcast journalism for a major television network. Conducting a multitiered job search means you would look at opportunities at regional stations and focus on the big players. Depending on the availability of positions, such an approach could also mean searching for opportunities that are closely related to what you really want. In this case, starting as a production assistant might be a great way to position yourself for the job you ultimately want.

When you decide to focus all your job search efforts on Plan A, you might be putting yourself at a disadvantage with your Plan B or Plan C if things don't come through. Why? Because it's going to be very difficult to convince a potential employer that you are truly interested in working for the company when you didn't spend any of your time networking with anyone there and you didn't apply for the position until just a few days before the application deadline. It's almost like holding out to ask the really cute girl or handsome guy to dance when you're out clubbing, only to have to approach someone you've passed over all night after getting turned down. Obviously, convincing someone you've been ignoring that you really wanted to be with him or her all along is going to be awfully hard, if not impossible.

I recently met with a client who applied to only two companies. He told me he didn't want to put all of his eggs in one basket. I replied "so you put all of your eggs in two baskets?" Even though it was multi-tiered, his strategy was still very risky.

On the other hand, whether you're looking for that special someone or for a job, you also don't need to feel as though you have to latch onto the first person or job opening that falls on your doorstep, or the reverse—that you have to hold out for "Mr./Ms. Right" or the perfect position. You also shouldn't just give up on a dream job because you think it's unattainable or will be too much of a challenge. That would be like deciding not to approach someone you're attracted to simply because you think that person is "out of your league."

Chapter 3

The Meet Market: Networking

"Anyone I meet, anyplace, anytime, if they can help me in some way, I'm game.
I wouldn't date my friend's older sister, but I'd definitely prod her for
career information."

—Carl, job seeker

Before you can date someone, you need to meet someone. And what better place to meet someone than the meet market? No, not the fine selection of steaks at your local grocery store or a bar full of obnoxious men or women who are busy undressing you with their eyes. I'm talking about meeting someone through a friend or a friend of a friend. In a poll conducted by *Cosmopolitan* magazine, women were asked "What's the best way to meet datable men?"[1] What was their number-one response? No, not approaching someone after last call at the local bar. "Through mutual friends." When you're looking for a job, mutual friends can

---

1. "Passion Poll: What's the Best Way to Meet Datable Men?" *Cosmopolitan*.
http://ivillage.opinionware.com/owuser/CommonOpinion?cmd=results&id=2/9/1494.
Accessed 16 June 2007.

also be a great resource for expanding your professional network. Tapping into your existing network of friends and family can be a great way to meet new contacts.

In fact, "personal contacts/networking" was the number-one most effective job search tactic reported by 78 percent of job seekers responding to a poll conducted by the Society for Human Resource Management.[2] "Employee referrals/employee referral programs" came in second, with 65 percent.

Even though many of us don't feel comfortable meeting new people in any setting, let alone while looking for jobs, doing so is a great way to gather career information and expand your personal network. According to Dr. Wayne Baker in *Achieving Success Through Social Capital,* your network of acquaintances and friends, or what he refers to as your "social capital," can lead to a number of positive outcomes, both personally and professionally. He writes, "Individuals who build and use social capital get better jobs, better pay, faster promotions, and are more influential and effective, compared with peers who are unable or unwilling to tap the power of social capital."[3] He means your networking skills will serve you well throughout your life.

Also keep in mind how much more comfortable it is to meet someone who's been introduced to you by a mutual friend. Even a blind date is easier if you and your date have mutual friends. Don't forget that when it's time to hire a new employee, most employers prefer to hire a job candidate who's been referred by a trusted employee. That way, they can feel more like they're venturing into known territory.

The Principles of Effective Networking

But how do you start building this "social capital"? Effective networking is a two-way street; it's just as important for you to help those in your network as it is for them to help you. I know, figuring out how you can help someone you've just met might sound difficult, but it's often easier than you think. You can offer to help connect the person with whom you're networking to someone in your network, or you

---

2. "Search Tactics Poll." Society for Human Resource Management. http://www.shrm. org/hrresources/surveys_published/Search%20Tactics%20Poll.asp#P-6_0. Accessed April 2001.

3. Wayne Baker. *Achieving Success Through Social Capital.* San Francisco: Jossey-Bass Inc., 2000. 25.

can offer to assist with a project. That being said, let's look at the key principles of effective networking.

- **Assess:** Whom do you know? Do your friends and acquaintances know each other? Contacts can be those you've met on the job as well as relatives, friends of relatives, personal friends, and acquaintances. You'll be surprised by how many people you already know directly or know through a friend or colleague. Some experts actually estimate we each have, on average, approximately 1,000 acquaintances. That number might seem high, but if you subscribe to the "Six Degrees of Kevin Bacon" theory, anyone on the planet can be connected to Kevin Bacon through a chain of acquaintances that has no more than five intermediaries. A number of mathematical experiments tend to support this theory.

- **Expand:** Continue to meet new people outside your existing network. They can be classmates or people you meet at work, in the community, or through a mutual friend. When you're going to school full time, devoting a lot of time to expanding your network can be hard. Try to dedicate an hour or two to meeting new people each week.

- **Maintain:** Remember, networking is about developing ongoing relationships, not just landing a job or an interview. Look for ways you can assist others in your network, whether it's by sharing information about an upcoming event they might be interested in or giving them a "heads up" about a potential job opening you've heard about. Think of the "social capital" or karma you gain when you lend a hand to friends. If you were ever in a position to introduce two single friends who hit it off, you know what I'm talking about.

While you're on the dating scene, or in this case expanding your network of contacts, leverage the skills and knowledge you've learned from past romantic relationships. Finding a job or internship is a lot like finding a boyfriend or girlfriend. Your success often depends on how much someone likes you, not necessarily on how smart or cute you are.

Meeting Other Singles: Expanding Your Career Network

Many of us have a difficult time figuring out where we can meet other singles even though they're already all around us. I've been able to meet plenty of people on the bus, waiting in line at the grocery store, or on a plane, and even though I'm not always looking for a job, getting to know people has been a great way to expand my social and professional networks.

In his book *Never Eat Alone,* author Keith Ferrazzi stresses the importance of meeting new people. "Sticking to the people we already know is a tempting behavior. But unlike some forms of dating, a networker isn't looking to achieve only a single successful union. Creating an enriching circle of trusted relationships requires one to be *out there,* in the mix, all the time."[4]

Where can you meet new people when you're looking for love or your dream job? My motto has always been "Everywhere but police stations and prisons"…unless you're considering a career in law enforcement, of course!

Your success rate will be much higher when you contact someone with whom you share a common interest. In the world of dating, think about how successful you would be if you just started randomly calling people in the phone book and asking them out on dates without some form of prior connection. The only conversations you'll be having will cost you about $2.99 per minute. The same holds true during your job search.

Using Your Connections

If you have access to your college or university alumni database, look for people doing what you are interested in. Fellow alumni are more inclined to talk to you than if you were a stranger because they already have something in common with you.

I once met with a client who was interested in a career in politics but felt he had no contacts to help him get started. When I asked him whether any of his family members worked in politics, he mentioned that his father was a high-ranking government official. What? How much more connected could he be? After further discussion, I found

---

4. Keith Ferrazzi with Tahl Raz. *Never Eat Alone.* New York: Doubleday, 2005. 50.

out that the client had decided not to talk to his father because he was worried that talking to him about job leads would be like asking him for a handout instead of a hand up.

That's not what networking is all about. In most cases, insiders are happy to help. If you end up taking a job at their company, they may very well be eligible for a hefty finder's fee. They may even enjoy seeing themselves as matchmakers—and if you've ever been the only single person in a large group of friends with mates, you know just how much people enjoy playing the matchmaker. But just as with dating, when you're networking, you have to assert yourself without being obnoxious or pushy. Passing out copies of your resume during a holiday dinner would be inappropriate, but talking to family members to gather career information and even job contacts and leads is perfectly acceptable behavior.

Chance Encounters

Chance encounters with people are also great ways to build or expand your career network. If sheer luck can help you meet new people in your personal life, it can also help you meet new people in your professional life. Of course, luck also requires you to assert yourself. You'll be amazed at the connections you can develop by talking to the people who are right under your nose. The hardest part for most people is figuring out how to start up a conversation with someone they've just met, but usually a pleasant greeting can lead to small talk about a common interest and things fall into place.

TIP: When you're following up with someone you met during a chance encounter, a great ice breaker can be as simple as a brief reminder of where and when you met.

Professional Associations

Professional associations exist for just about any field of work. Examples include the National Athletic Trainers' Association, the American Astronomical Society, the American Society of Landscape Architects, and the National Association of Sales Professionals. They often encourage *prospective* members to attend events. They also hold annual conferences for members that, once you become a member, would give you exposure to hundreds, if not thousands, of potential contacts. Tapping into the vast resources at the disposal of each member of such associations can assist you immeasurably in uncovering opportunities and gaining an advantage over the competition in your job search.

TIP: For a comprehensive list of detailed information including addresses and descriptions for more than 20,000 professional associations, check your local library for the *Encyclopedia of Associations: National Organizations of the U.S.* published by Thomson Gale.

Online Social and Professional Networking

In addition to expanding your personal and professional networks through friends, family, and chance encounters, there are a number of very effective Web tools available to help you meet new people.

Personal Sites

To expand your personal network, consider the following:

- **Facebook** (www.facebook.com): Facebook is a rapidly growing online community that connects college and high school students through social networks. You can look up people at your school, see how people know each other, and post personal interests.

  - Pros: Rapidly growing community on a lot of college campuses.

  - Cons: Not just for college students anymore.

- **Friendster** (www.friendster.com): Created in 2003, Friendster is an online community designed to help you organize your social life. With more than 13 million members, Friendster enables users to stay connected with friends, meet new people through their friends, and see how their friends are connected to each other.

  - Pros: More than 40 million members, career focused, and free (for now).

  - Cons: Lack of enough career-focused features.

- **MySpace** (www.myspace.com): A recent article on CNN.com reported that MySpace.com now has 2½ times the traffic of Google.[5] Think about that for a second. When you do, it should come as no surprise that MySpace recently passed Friendster as the top social-networking Web site. MySpace is a free online community designed to help you meet your friends' friends. Whether you're single and looking to meet that special someone, or you're looking for a job and want to network with businesspeople, MySpace can help you connect through a growing network of mutual friends. The site also has a blog, discussion forum, groups, and classifieds.

  - Pros: Free (for now).

  - Cons: Lack of enough career-focused features.

Professional Sites

To expand your professional network, consider the following:

- **LinkedIn** (www.linkedin.com): LinkedIn is a career-focused networking tool used by more than 11 million professionals to locate and connect with industry experts and business partners. You can search the network on a number of criteria including keyword, location, company, job title, person's name, and industry. LinkedIn also offers a relationship-powered job network that allows members to search openings and uncover connections to recruiters, HR managers, and hiring managers.

  - Pros: Free (for now) and widely used by a lot of people.

  - Cons: Designed more for experienced professionals.

- **Monster Networking** (http://network.monster.com): Monster Networking is a career-focused networking tool that allows you to search for contacts by keyword and geographic area. The site also offers industry-specific message boards and expert-led discussions. Member profiles include location, gender, job title, employment history, educational background, and other information such as skills and interests.

---

5. "MySpace's the Place Online." CNN.com. www.cnn.com/2006/TECH/internet/02/13/rising.onlinespace.ap/index.html. Accessed 13 February 2006.

- Pros: Career focus and a strong brand.

- Cons: Need to have a subscription to create connections.

- **Ryze** (www.ryze.com): Ryze helps people make connections and grow their personal and professional networks. Members can also join special career networks related to their industry, interest, and geographic preferences.

  - Pros: Free basic access including a home page and special career-related networks.

  - Cons: Not as well known as other sites; advanced features require a subscription.

A Caveat

The preceding sites are primarily for networking/finding jobs or for meeting other singles—of course, not at the same time. If you're looking for jobs, make sure the information you share online is appropriate and professional at all times. You never know who might see the personal information and opinions you're putting out there. This means no provocative pictures in bikinis or Speedos.

Over the past few weeks, I've seen a number of articles highlighting the dangers associated with sharing personal information on social networking sites. Similar to fears people had about chat rooms a few years back, the primary concern is over the possibility of online predators using the sites to target unsuspecting victims. Whether such behavior is or does become an epidemic remains to be seen. Either way, being careful about what you share online is a good idea. Once you put something out there, it's out there. There aren't any take-backs or mulligans. You wouldn't want someone to stumble across personal information or controversial opinions you've posted online that could hurt your chances with a company with which you'd like to interview.

Dating Do's and Don'ts: Effective Networking Tips

This section presents some essential networking do's and don'ts. You'll learn how to break the ice, make technology work for you, introduce yourself effectively, and never forget to say thanks to people who help you along the way.

Ice Breakers Part 2

Regardless of whether you're shy or out-going, ice breakers come in handy when you meet someone new. I'm not talking "You must be tired because you've been running through my mind all day." Rather, something more along the lines of "Hi, my name is *[insert your name here]*. What's your name?"

When you're networking, it's also a good idea to have some conversation starters— what some people like to refer to as a "60-second conversation" or "elevator speech." You can use your job search introduction, or what I like to refer to as ice breakers, when you're networking or when you're approaching a recruiter at a company presentation or career fair. This opener is called a "60-second conversation" or "elevator speech" because it's meant to enable you to grab someone's attention in the time it would take to ride with that person in an elevator. However, I think "ice breaker" is more accurate because your conversations will rarely be 60-second, uninterrupted narratives or elevator speeches. If they are, you're going to spend that time talking *at* the person instead of talking *with* him or her.

> *I think that it is important to be talkative and outgoing without being overbearing and cocky. For example, while on a date, one shouldn't dominate conversation and talk about [oneself] all the time. Likewise, during a job search, when meeting with potential employers, it is important to pick and choose the right times to talk.*
>
> —Alex, investment banking analyst

An effective introduction includes your name, the type of work or internship you're looking for, a brief overview of your related experience (if applicable), and a highlight of relevant skills you possess. (See the sample script for a 60-second conversation or elevator speech later in this section.) Practice your introduction until you feel comfortable with your delivery but try to avoid memorizing your introduction word for word. Doing so could make the conversation seem forced or rehearsed. Plus, if the person you're speaking with interrupts you or switches things around, you could be thrown off track.

There are some additional practical steps you can take to make networking easier and more effective. For example, practice talking to friends and family first. By interacting with people you know, you can gain confidence in a controlled environment. Over time, you'll find that the more you talk to people, the easier it becomes. Eventually, you'll also want to get feedback from people who don't know you as well as your friends and family, who might overlook or not notice some of your little idiosyncrasies.

Sample Script: 60-Second Conversation

The elevator doors open....

Internship seeker: Good afternoon.

Employer: Hi, how are you?

Internship seeker: Great. It looks like you're headed to a meeting.

Employer: Yes. We have one every Monday morning at 9.

Internship seeker: What line of work are you in?

Employer: I work in advertising for Jackson Laugton. What brings you here today?

Internship seeker: I am majoring in journalism and mass communications at Boston University, and I am in New York meeting with alumni to discuss possible internship opportunities.

Employer: What firms are you meeting with?

Internship seeker: AAA Advertising and Smith & Co. Unfortunately, I wasn't able to set anything up with Jackson Laugton. Is there anyone you can think of that I can meet with while I'm in town?

Employer: Yes. In fact, one of my colleagues was just talking about hiring an intern. If you have a copy of your resume, I'd be happy to pass it along.

Internship seeker: I do; here you go. Thank you for offering to forward my resume. Do you happen to have a business card? I would like to follow up with you if that's okay.

Also consider pairing up with friends and family members who are more comfortable networking at career fairs and other recruiting events. Not only will you be able to observe and learn from their individual networking styles and techniques, but they'll also be there to provide moral support and to help you break the ice when meeting new people. It's like having a wing-man—a good friend who makes introductions and talks you up to guys or girls in the dating world.

Don't Drop a Call

Before you start reaching out and meeting new people, make sure you have a professional-sounding voice mail. Believe it or not, "I'm busy watching television, leave a message" or including a crazy background track won't get you the kinds of messages you want when you're looking for a job. And if you happen to have a roommate, make sure he or she doesn't change your message to something unprofessional. Once, when I was in college, my roommate changed my voice-mail message without telling me...and it was absolutely terrible. I was in the middle of the campus recruiting season, and his message was filled with so much profanity, it definitely would have cost me any hope of interviewing with any company that heard it. I'm not sure what possessed him to do that, but luckily a friend told me about it, and I was able to change it before any damage was done. For more networking do's and don'ts, check out table 3.1.

Table 3.1: Networking Do's and Don'ts

Networking Do's	Networking Don'ts
Be professional and courteous in all your interactions.	Make a contact feel used or manipulated.
Proofread all e-mails.	Ask a contact to find you a job.
Ask insightful and thoughtful questions.	Send generic e-mails to new or existing contacts.
Ask for names of others who may be willing to help you.	Come off sounding desperate.
Send thank-you notes to contacts whether or not they were helpful.	Send a copy of your resume.
Follow up with contacts who haven't responded.	Miss or be late to a meeting.
Stay in touch with contacts even after you've found a job.	Abuse relationships.
	Monopolize someone's time when he or she has agreed to speak with you.

Having a professional-caliber e-mail address is also very important to a successful job search. In other words, *wonderstud@aol.com* or *sugarbear@yahoo.com* (believe it or not, I've actually seen an e-mail address similar to this on a resume) aren't options unless you want to be a carpenter or a platinum recording artist. I know, you *are* a wonder stud or diva and you want to tell the world, but using an unprofessional-sounding e-mail address can definitely lead to a negative first impression, which may be the only impression the employer ever gets of you. If necessary, create one e-mail address such as *firstname.lastname@gmail.com* to use with your job search and one to use for personal matters. If you have a job but you're applying for openings at other companies, steer clear of using your current work e-mail address on your resume or to send or receive e-mails related to your job search. Personally, I think listing your work e-mail looks unprofessional. Plus, some employers might consider it an inappropriate use of their technology to send or receive e-mails relating to your job search. I think most employers would agree, when you're at work, you should be working, not looking for other jobs. If you need to e-mail or call someone about a job, use a personal e-mail account or cell phone and contact that person during your lunch break or after work.

If you are going to be out of town or away from your computer for a few days, be sure to set an "out of office" message on your e-mail account. That way, professional contacts or potential employers won't think you're a slacker or that you're avoiding them if you don't respond immediately (I define *immediately* as "within 24 hours") to their e-mail message.

Do your best to stay connected. Check your voice mail and e-mail as much as you can, even when you're on vacation. Most hotels offer high-speed Internet access for $10 to $12 per night. If you're not able to connect from your hotel room, try to locate a FedEx Kinko's in your area. Remember, lots of great candidates are vying for jobs out there. If a company doesn't hear back from you in a few days, chances are it will hire someone else.

Introduction Seduction

As you reach out to people you haven't met before, be sure to mention how you found their contact information during your introduction. In some cases, you'll need to remind them how you met in the first place. This strategy will not only help to avoid any confusion on their part, but will also enable you to differentiate yourself from other potential job seekers, especially when you were referred by someone they are familiar with.

During conversations, pay close attention to what the person is saying as well as how she or he is saying it. Nonverbal signals can tell you a lot about a person's interest in talking with you. If you're on a date and the person you're with seems interested in your conversation, you keep going. However, if you notice your date dozing off, no longer making eye contact, or frequently glancing at his or her watch, you ask for the check. The same holds true when you're networking. If you notice the person you're speaking with doesn't seem interested, wrap up the conversation and conclude by sincerely thanking the person and wishing him or her a nice day. And keep adding to your list of contacts. Each time you find people you hit it off with, ask them for a business card at the end of your conversation so that you can follow up with them in the future. Think of this part of the job search as being similar to exchanging telephone numbers with someone you meet at a club—kind of awkward, but a necessary first step. Sometimes you'll get rejected by people who aren't willing to share their contact information. Other times you'll meet people who will want to help you with your job or internship search.

Don't Forget to Say Thanks

Send thank-you notes to people you speak with, whether or not they bent over backwards to assist you. After all, it is a small world, and you never know when you will run into the same people in the future. A thank-you note is like sending flowers to someone you're dating: It quite often leaves a lasting impression. Plus, when is the last time someone sent you a thank-you note for anything that didn't cost money? It doesn't happen often, and it is a great way for you to make yourself stand out.

TIP: I know this should go without saying, but never, and I repeat *never*, send flowers to someone with whom you've interviewed. I actually had someone ask me if it would be okay to send an interviewer flowers as a nice thank you. Maybe if he wanted to work for a florist, but it's a really bad move for all other companies because it will make you look totally desperate (not to mention creepy).

Thank-you notes can be sent via e-mail, or they can be typed letters or handwritten notes. The method you select depends heavily on the industry you're dealing with and the context of the relationship you've established with the recipient. For example, people working in marketing or advertising are more creative and might be more receptive to a handwritten note, whereas someone working in the information technology industry might prefer an e-mail message.

Thank-you letters typically contain three brief paragraphs (two to three sentences each) meant to thank someone for taking time to speak with you. Don't dilute the message by asking for further assistance; the purpose of such a letter is simply to thank the recipient. (See figure 3.1 for a sample.)

```
Dear Mary:

Thank you for taking time to speak with me on Friday, March 4.

Your insights and advice on how I can best position myself for
a career in retail management are greatly appreciated. I also
enjoyed learning more about the exciting initiatives GatorMart
is currently undertaking.

Thank you again for your time and consideration.

Sincerely,
Sara Student
```

Figure 3.1: Sample networking e-mail thank-you message.

In the first paragraph, you can thank the person for his or her time on the particular occasion you spoke. List the exact date instead of saying "it was a pleasure speaking with you last week" because you never know when the person will receive the letter or read it. Plus, including the date is more formal and businesslike. In the second paragraph, you can recap a particular point from your discussion. You could say something like, "I appreciated your advice regarding the best way to position myself for a career in retail management." Specific details from the discussion (proof of your active listening), along with, perhaps, a very brief reference to your plans to benefit from it, are also appropriate. Use the final paragraph to thank the person again for his or her time and consideration. (See chapter 8 for more information about sending thank-you notes after job interviews.)

TIP: Each person you contact will most likely differ in his or her willingness to assist you in your job search. You'll be surprised how many people are more than happy to talk to you about their career. This helpful attitude isn't universal, however.

If you are faced with a situation in which someone isn't interested in talking to you, don't give up. Try to salvage the interaction by asking the person you're speaking with to refer you to someone else. The worst thing he or she can say is no, and if you're lucky, you can be introduced to a new networking contact.

Swapping Digits: Reaching Out to Employers and Networking Contacts

Meeting people is obviously the first step to building your network. But it's not the only step. Your ability to follow up with contacts will go a long way to building a rapport with them. Don't be afraid to ask for a business card. And once you do, be sure your follow-up is prompt and professional. Let's take a look at strategies for doing both.

Always Get a Number

When you hit it off with someone you'd like to ask out, you ask for his or her number. If the interest is mutual, you add each other's numbers to your respective cell phones. When you hit it off with someone you're networking with, requesting a business card is just like asking for his or her number. Better than swapping digits, getting a business card allows you to jot down important notes about your meeting or conversation without having to worry about relying on your memory to keep track of details. On the back of the card, write down where you met the person and the date of the meeting, along with any information on where the person is from or what she or he is interested in. We all like to think that we're memorable. If you take the time to remember details about a person, you appear that much more impressive when you reach out to that person later.

Avoid Follow-Up Faux Pas

E-mail will most likely play a large part in your communications with employers and networking contacts, so it's important that you take time to make sure your messages don't have any grammatical errors and that they sound professional. It's easy to let your guard down and send a quick e-mail to a recruiter that could end up hurting or ending your candidacy. One of the most common mistakes I see people make occurs when they cut and paste content from one e-mail to another. Often, they'll forget to change the name of the person they are e-mailing in their introduction, or they'll list the wrong company name, date, or position title. Spell-checking software will catch most typos, but it won't catch the errors I just mentioned. That's why it is important for you to read each e-mail to yourself before you send it out. Or ask a friend to go over it with a fine-toothed comb.

Because we rely so heavily on e-mail, I often meet with clients who forget that there are other ways to reach out to contacts during their job search. I've spoken with plenty of job seekers who've sent multiple e-mails over a period of weeks but don't know what to do when they don't get a response from a particular contact. I always recommend calling to follow up with those who haven't responded a week or two after you sent the e-mail. Let's face it, it's easy to accidentally delete an e-mail or have it get lost in the in-box. Plus, you never know whether the person you're trying to contact would rather touch base over the phone rather than respond to an e-mail. By using a combination of e-mails and phone calls when following up with leads, you're increasing your chances of getting a response.

But if you're going to call, make sure you think through what you're going to say before you pick up that phone. A great example of what can go wrong when you don't takes place in the movie *Swingers* (hands down the single best movie for surviving a breakup ever). On the rebound from a painful breakup, Mike (played by Jon Favreau) gets up the nerve to approach a woman at a bar. They strike up a conversation, and she gives him her number. When Mike gets home, he decides to give her a call. He gets her answering machine and, being really nervous, he rambles on and on. Before he can leave his call-back number, the machine cuts him off. In a panic, he decides to call and leave her another message. He again gets cut off and calls back. After five or so phone calls in a matter of 30 seconds, she finally picks up the phone and tells him not to call again...ever! It's just as easy to look like a dork when you're calling someone about a possible job or internship.

To keep this from happening, type out what you're going to say or write it out on a note card. Read it through once or twice and then make the call. Keep your script in front of you in case you need to refer to it. Always remember to start your message by mentioning your name and phone number at the outset and then repeat them before you hang up. If you've left a message but that person hasn't immediately responded, try waiting at least five days before following up again. That way, if the person is out of the office or swamped with work, he or she will have adequate time to contact you. Waiting to hear back from someone can be stressful, but you don't want to ruin a possible networking relationship by being a pest and calling too often. As long as you're professional and succinct, people generally don't mind a follow-up phone call.

Keep Track of Contacts

Keeping track of everyone you talk to can be difficult, but when you're looking for a job (or a mate, for that matter), being able to do so is critical. To manage your contacts, consider creating a spreadsheet, using an online resource such as Plaxo (www.plaxo.com), or writing them down in a notebook. Include as much information as possible about each contact, such as the person's name, title, employer, address, telephone number, e-mail, your connection with him or her, and any miscellaneous information you feel is important.

Including a "Next Steps" column in your contacts spreadsheet enables you to stay on top of your search by clearly outlining action items to address in the near future. Say, for example, you contact someone who is too busy to talk, and that person asks you to call back on Friday. If you don't keep track of the date you need to follow up, it could very easily slip your mind. (See figure 3.2 for a sample contact-management spreadsheet.)

Name	Title	Organization	Address	City/State/ZIP	Phone	E-mail	Contact Date	Next Steps
Joe Public	Assistant Manager	Acme Company	1234 Street	Anycity/PA/15213	412-555-0000	jpublic@acme.com	10/3	Send thank-you letter.
Toni Smith	Executive Director	CRT Designs	44 E. Avenue	Anycity/PA/15213	412-555-1111	tsmith@crt.com	10/5	Left message. Call back 10/14
Paul Gadola	Account Manager	Gadola & Co.	10 Boulevard	Anycity/PA/15213	412-555-2222	paul.gadola@gandc.com	10/8	Schedule informational interview.

Figure 3.2: A sample contact-management spreadsheet.

Chapter 4

Physical Attraction: Creating Eye-Catching Resumes and Cover Letters

Hot, drop-dead gorgeous, beautiful, handsome. Words you might use to describe someone you pass on the street or meet at a club. Whether or not we want to admit it, physical attraction plays a huge role in whether we ask someone out or say yes when someone asks us out. And in most cases, it has to. After all, we see the physical before we have a chance to get to know the individual. When it comes to your job search, physical attraction is just as important. Instead of good looks or a hot body, employers decide whether they want to interview you based on how attracted they are to your resume, cover letter, skills, and personality.

Creating Attractive Resumes

Visually appealing resumes that are easy to read will stand out in a crowd like a hot guy or girl stands out from a bunch of "Average Joes" or "Average Janes." Over the years, I've critiqued thousands of resumes for students, and in so doing, I've found that most people don't know what an attractive resume looks like. I've also found that few people are qualified to edit their own resumes without seeking any second or third opinions. I once reviewed a resume that was a copy of a copy of a copy and was next to impossible to read. I've also seen my fair share of resumes with inconsistent formatting and typos. To make sure your resume is going to stand out, consider the following questions:

- Is the format attractive and easy to read?

- Is it free of typos? Are you sure?

- Are the margins and font size consistent?

- Did you focus on results and accomplishments?

- Would you consider the resume if you were a recruiter?

Chances are, the person who'll be accepting or rejecting your resume works in Human Resources and spends a majority of his or her time scanning dozens, if not hundreds, of resumes per day. Think about how you can make your resume stand out from a pile of similar resumes. I hope the thing that differentiates yours from the others won't be a coffee stain from breakfast. Your resume can say a lot about who you are, including whether you are an organized person and whether you pay attention to detail.

There are two basic resume formats: chronological and skills/functional or combination. Both should include your contact information, educational background, and work experience (including the dates of each). Some people also list additional information such as certifications, computer skills, and hobbies. This information may be quite appropriate, even essential, if it's job-related. But your age, height, weight, and marital status should never be included. Also, unless you are aspiring to be a professional model, don't include your photo anywhere on your resume. You'll get to show off your good looks during the interview. See figure 4.1 for a general resume template, and later figures for examples of the different resume types.

Name
Address
Phone number(s)
E-mail address

OBJECTIVE

Optional. Indicates the type of position for which you are looking; should be concise.

EDUCATION

YOUR UNIVERSITY
Bachelor of Arts—Your Major, Graduation Month, Year
List GPA if 3.0 or higher. Can also list classes if experience is limited.

Study-Abroad University, Seville, Spain   Spring 20XX

EXPERIENCE

MOST RECENT EMPLOYER
Your title   Month Year–Month Year
- Describe your experience with phrases and by function.
- Emphasize significant achievements, results produced, and recognition from others.
- Begin phrases with action verbs.
- Quantify accomplishments when possible and use specific examples.

PREVIOUS EMPLOYER
Your title   Month Year–Month Year
-
-
-

HONORS

Include academic honors such as scholarships, the Dean's List, and honor societies.

ACTIVITIES

- List offices held, organizations, projects, and skills and abilities utilized.
- Include activities and interests that show leadership or initiative, or Relate to the position for which you are applying.
- Spell out acronyms.

Figure 4.1: Resume template.

Guy or Girl Next Door: The Chronological Resume Format

As down-to-earth as the guy or girl next door, the chronological format makes up for its lack of flash and pizzazz with its substance. In this format, experience is listed in reverse-chronological order, with your most recent employment listed first. Of the two resume formats, chronological is the one more commonly used and most often expected.

The following sections give details on how to put together the different sections of your chronological resume. Figures 4.2 and 4.3 show samples.

Katherine Student
1000 Oak Place
Wilson, NC 27896
(919) 555-2400 • Cell: (919) 555-1400
katie.student@unc.edu

EDUCATION	*UNIVERSITY OF NORTH CAROLINA AT CHAPEL HILL* **School of Journalism and Mass Communication** Bachelor of Arts, May 2008 Public Relations sequence; History minor
EXPERIENCE	REX HEALTHCARE, Raleigh, NC ***Public Relations and Marketing Intern,*** January 2008–May 2008 • Wrote press releases about hospital events, awards, and achievements. • Assisted marketing coordinators with campaigns for cardiovascular, seniors, and women's health accounts. • Wrote copy for brochures and fact sheets. • Communicated directly with local media about press releases and assisted with on-site media events. • Created surveys to assess the quality of Rex Lactation Services. • Redesigned RexWebMD and presented revisions to Physician Satisfaction team.

BLUE & WHITE MAGAZINE, UNIVERSITY OF NORTH CAROLINA, Chapel Hill, NC
Publisher, May 2007–February 2008
• Oversaw magazine's financial and business affairs.
• Created a $12,000 budget for the magazine.
• Presented to Student Congress to obtain additional funding for the magazine.

Associate Publisher for Marketing, May 2006–May 2007
• Directed planning of special events, such as a 5K fund-raiser and Student Body President debate.
• Organized distribution of the magazine and other publicity efforts each month.
• Supervised the 10-member marketing team.

Special Events Manager, May 2005–May 2006
• Planned the first *Blue & White* 5K fund-raiser.
• Organized all monthly "pit events" to aid in publicity and distribution of the magazine.
• Created flyers publicizing each new issue of the magazine.

Communications Assistant—School of Information and Library Science, August 2006–May 2007
• Wrote press releases about school-related special events, faculty news, and awards.
• Wrote feature articles about faculty, alumni, and other events for a biannual alumni newsletter.
• Updated School of Information and Library Science website, www.ils.unc.edu.

WILSON DAILY TIMES, Wilson, NC
News Intern, August 2002–January 2006
• Wrote three to five stories weekly for a newspaper serving approximately 30,000 readers.
• Awarded "Best Story of the Quarter" for a feature story.
• Wrote two articles accepted by The Associated Press and published in seven newspapers throughout North Carolina.

COMPUTER SKILLS	Proficient: Microsoft Word, Works, Excel, and PowerPoint Knowledgeable: HTML, Dreamweaver, and Photoshop

Figure 4.2: A sample chronological resume.

Formatting Tips

Here are some tips on formatting your resume:

- Margins should be uniform around the page, with a minimum of a half-inch and a maximum of 1 inch.

- Times New Roman is the most common font used for resumes, with Arial also being very popular. Unless you're applying for openings in an industry looking for someone very creative (such as advertising, marketing, and entertainment), it's a bad idea to choose an artsy font, such as Comic Sans; for most jobs, your resume needs to look formal and conservative.

- Font size for all text should be the same and range between 10.5 and 12 points, depending on how much information you have and what font style you select. With Times New Roman, you can usually squeeze a lot more words into a smaller space than you can with Arial or any other sans-serif font.

- Your name can be a larger font than the rest of the resume, but it shouldn't exceed 18 points.

Contact Info

Contact information should always be listed first. If you're a college student, you can list your current school address and a permanent address, but be sure to indicate which one is which. Everyone else should list one address. Your name, address, telephone number, and e-mail address should always be included in this first section. You can also list a mobile phone number and your personal Web site (but be sure there's nothing embarrassing on it).

If you list your mobile phone number, be aware that you may receive a call when you are at a crowded restaurant or at some other inopportune time. To keep this from happening, let calls from numbers you don't recognize or that appear on caller ID as unknown go to voice mail. That way, you can return them when you have time to gather your composure and adequately prepare.

Listing a personal Web site is almost never a good idea unless you're applying for a computer software position. If you do list a site or a relevant blog, it should look professional and not contain any offensive material, such as inappropriate images, language, or other content. And you should also consider whether anything in the content might alienate a future employer.

Objective

In most cases, you will outline your objective in your cover letter, so including one on your resume is optional. If you list an objective, don't use fluff. Anyone can say he or she would like to work in a challenging environment with opportunities for advancement. This could mean an entry-level job as a restroom attendant with an opportunity to move into a position as restroom attendant management. (No offense to all the hardworking restroom attendants out there…but you get my point.) Instead, list the position title or function of interest (for example, brand management position in consumer packaged goods).

Education

For current college students or recent graduates, education normally comes first after contact information. You'll want to list your most recent or current college or university first. You don't need to list your high school in this section, unless you're a high school student looking for a summer job or your first job after graduation. When you list college and professional degrees, include the following:

- The name of your school
- Its location
- Degree received
- Any honors (such as magna cum laude)
- Your graduation date
- Your major and relevant minors

Depending on the type of job you're applying for, this section or a following section might be the best place to list any professional articles or books you've had published. If professional publications aren't important in your target career, you should still list any publications in the final section, where you list peripheral skills and qualifications. After all, writing is one of the most highly valued skills in the job market.

Experience

Unless your work experience is more of a selling point for you than your educational background, the Experience section comes next, after Education. Listing jobs you held in high school is not as important once you land your first full-time, permanent position. If you can list every job, do it, because gaps in employment often send up a red flag. The problem with gaps is that they can potentially make you look lazy, unfocused, or even like you're hiding something (such as prison time).

For each job, list the name of the organization, its location, the dates you worked, your title, and your responsibilities. Because recruiters spend a limited amount of time reviewing each individual resume, it is critically important that the information you list for each position you've held stands out. Using bullet points to outline your major accomplishments enables the reader to scan the resume quickly without having to dig for information. When possible, each bullet should relate to the job you're applying for and focus on a positive result that occurred because of your contributions. Use plenty of action verbs (a comprehensive list is available in the appendix) when describing what you did while on the job. For example, instead of saying, "I was a recruiter for Acme Corporation," say, "Recruited management-level consultants" or something equally detailed and leave out the "I."

What's the Deal with CVs?

Some quick facts on CVs:

- A CV, or curriculum vitae, is typically used for academic positions at the Ph.D. level or for jobs outside the United States.

- A CV is similar to a resume in that it provides an overview of your work experience and academic background.

- Unlike most traditional resumes, CVs include an exhaustive list of publications, conference presentations, and other evidence of scholarly work.

- Length can vary from two pages for a new professional to 10 pages for a person with extensive experience.

If you've held jobs that weren't related to the types of positions you're applying for, or even jobs you wish you'd never held, there are ways you can minimize the amount of attention drawn to those jobs on your resume. For example, say you were a server at a restaurant for six months when you were between jobs. You can list experience related to the positions you're applying for in a Related Experience section. Then include your time as a server in an Other Experience category near the bottom of your resume. This will allow you to group your experiences out of reverse-chronological order based on their relevance to the positions you're applying for. In the Other Experience category, you can still list the name of the company and your title if you want, but you don't have to provide a breakdown of your job duties. That way, you'll be able to include descriptions for the positions that are most relevant without having to include bullets like "Operated cash register" from your time as a server.

NOTE: If you've had a job you're totally ashamed of, it's up to you to decide whether leaving a gap on your resume is better than including the job in question.

JOHN STUDENT
jstudent@email.unc.edu

SCHOOL ADDRESS:
107 Pritchard Avenue
Chapel Hill, NC 27516
919.555.1111

HOME ADDRESS:
1000 Buhl Avenue
Memphis, TN 38104
901.555.2222

EDUCATION
UNIVERSITY OF NORTH CAROLINA AT CHAPEL HILL
Bachelor of Arts in History, May 2008
Cumulative GPA: 3.32

HONORS
Dean's List
Sigma Chi Alumni Scholarship—all semesters

EXPERIENCE
ACME TRAFFIC SERVICES, Chapel Hill, NC
Co-Owner and Operator, Fall 2006–Spring 2008
- Started a business projected to gross over $10,000 in first year of operation.
- Maintained accurate accounting records for tax and payroll purposes.
- Marketed business to potential clients.
- Successfully completed engagements, securing repeat customers.
- Set up a branch site in Memphis, TN, under a commission paid employee.

GTX, INC., Memphis, TN
Financial Assistant, Summers 2006–2007
- Assisted in documentation to support private financing rounds.
- Exposed to the process of preparing for a biotech initial public offering.
- Participated in development of cash-flow forecasts using Excel.

Lab Technician, Summer 2005
- Compiled data from an experiment testing an oral medication.
- Calibrated instruments for Quality Assurance analysis.

LEADERSHIP
EXPERIENCE
SIGMA CHI FRATERNITY, Chapel Hill, NC
Social Chairman, Fall 2006–Spring 2007
- Controlled a $12,000 budget each semester and coordinated events.

Intramural Chairman, Fall 2004–Spring 2006
- Secured participation of 60 members for 10 intramural sports.

CAMPUS
ACTIVITIES
Carolina Entrepreneurial Club
Dance Marathon
Intramural Sports

COMPUTER
SKILLS
Microsoft Word, Excel, PowerPoint, QuickBooks

Figure 4.3: Another sample chronological resume.

Don't Front

In the world of dating, we all know how much trouble people can get into when they lie to impress someone. For example, you tell someone you attended a small, prestigious prep school, only to find out the person you're talking to attended the same small, prestigious prep school during the time you said you were there.

To avoid any confusion during your job search, don't exaggerate or lie about your skills and experience. I once worked with a student whose resume indicated he was fluent in Spanish. In reality, he had barely attained a conversational level. During an interview, the recruiter started speaking Spanish, and the student wasn't able to keep the conversation going. Remember, anything you list on your resume can be placed under the microscope during the interview process. This includes your academic background, experience, and skills. If you don't believe me, ask the former head football coach at Notre Dame, the former CEO of RadioShack, and the former dean of admissions at MIT—all of whom had to resign following questions about the accuracy of their resumes.

You should always assume that someone will check your references. It's quite common for a representative of the hiring company to call to verify graduation and degree information, for example. And people do get caught, all the time. According to ADP Screening and Selection Services, "51% of employment, education and/or credential reference checks revealed a difference of information between what the applicant provided and the source reported."[1]

Specialized Skills/Additional Data

The final section of a typical resume consists of any specialized skills or qualifications that weren't listed earlier. This category can include computer skills, specialized training, certifications and licensure, club memberships, language fluency, and community service. This section will vary based on the type of position you're applying for. Its main purpose is to flesh out your qualifications for a position with non-compensated experience or seemingly unrelated, but still important, skills. If you speak or read a foreign language, you can include that information here. The company might be looking for a sales professional to take over an account with a Japanese firm, and your Japanese-language skills might be just the ticket. But never exaggerate your facility with a foreign language.

TIP: Contrary to popular belief, concluding your resume with "References Available upon Request" isn't necessary because it's assumed that you will be able and willing to provide references at the company's request.

1. "Hire Insight Newsletter: Fall 2003." Automatic Data Processing Inc.
https://ox.avert.com/apps/pdf/hireInsightFall03.pdf.

He's Smart and He's Good Looking: The Combination Resume Format

Don't we all wish we could find someone we consider to be both hot and intelligent? What a combination. Maybe someone who was a cross between Jessica Simpson and Albert Einstein, or Colin Farrell and Maya Angelou. When it comes to resumes, the combination format is just that: It combines the chronological format with a highlight of the skills you have to offer. When would you use this format? When you want the recruiter to focus more on your skills and abilities than on the organizations you worked for. For example, I once counseled a 25-year-old client who worked as a repossession agent (in my opinion, one of the coolest jobs around) but was looking for a job in another industry. Something that didn't involve getting shot at on a daily basis. He wanted to flesh out his transferable skills without tying them to his previous job, which had some negative connotations.

N O T E : The combination resume uses the best features of the chronological resume (an in-order listing of the jobs you've held) and the skills resume (a topic-centered account of the skills you have that are relevant to the job). Employers tend to dislike skills resumes that omit a chronological jobs list, so avoid using that format unless you have huge time gaps in your experience or you have no actual relevant experience.

This format is also effective for those who have had a large number of jobs over a short period of time. It enables you to bundle the experience that's most closely related to the job you're applying for instead of listing it in reverse-chronological order.

Here are the primary elements of a combination resume and where they go:

- **Contact info:** A combination resume still needs to place contact information up front.

- **Skills:** As mentioned previously, with a combination resume, you'll want to group your experience based on skills, not the dates your experience occurred. Sample Skills category headings can include the following: Marketing, Management, Communication, Creativity, Writing, and any other headings you feel highlight skills the employer is looking for. Look at each job description to get a feel for which skills the company thinks are most important and then organize your skills accordingly. If marketing is listed near the end of the job description and management is listed first, your headings should follow suit.

- **Education:** Similar to the chronological format, in the Education section of a combination resume you'll want to list your most recent or current college or university first. Again, unless you're a high school student looking for a summer job or your first job after graduation, you don't need to list your high school in this section. When you list college and professional degrees, include the name of your school, degree, and any honors you received.

- **Experience:** For recent college graduates, the Experience section comes after Skills and Education. If you've been out of college more than five years, you can move Education further down your resume. Unlike the chronological format, with a combination resume, your Experience section won't describe prior job duties and accomplishments. Instead, include only company names, job titles, and the dates you were employed at each organization.

Figure 4.4 shows a combination resume appropriate for a health services job in a hospital or an extended-care facility. Notice that the job seeker emphasizes his management, communication, and customer service skills, which are likely to be a part of the job he's seeking.

What's the Deal with Video Resumes?

The name says it all. With video resumes, job seekers highlight their skills and accomplishments in front of a camera instead of on paper. There's been a lot of buzz about them and many career experts think they're the next big thing. But, unless you're applying for an interactive media position or something in the entertainment industry, I'm not sold, for three primary reasons:

- **Consistency of content will be difficult.** Many job seekers still struggle with preparing a professional-caliber hard-copy resume, and that's without the complexity of also serving as a videographer and personal stylist.

- **Companies need to be able to query and store your resume.** Most don't have the infrastructure to do that with video resumes yet.

- **It opens you up for possible discrimination issues.** You want recruiters to evaluate your candidacy based on your interaction with them during your interview, not based on how you present yourself on a short video.

STEVEN M. SMITH
34 Clayton Road
Concord, CA 94520
925-555-5555
ssmith237@excite.net

SKILLS

MANAGEMENT
- Supervised and scheduled a staff of approximately 50 employees.
- Resolved and documented all employee personnel issues.
- Conducted sanitation and safety inspections to ensure department meets or exceeds JCAHO standards.
- Developed and conducted training and in-services for all departmental staff.
- Participated in interviewing, hiring, performance evaluations, and termination of employees.
- Monitored and maintained departmental inventory levels.

COMMUNICATION
- Created and enforced Dietary Department policies and procedures.
- Planned and prepared menus for special events.
- Prepared and submitted financial reports.
- Counseled patients on drug-nutrient interactions.
- Conducted general health and nutritional information seminars for community members.

CUSTOMER SERVICE
- Ensured high level of customer satisfaction by providing prompt, friendly service.
- Interacted with sales representatives, doctors, and other constituencies.

EXPERIENCE

CONTRA COSTA REGIONAL MEDICAL CENTER, Martinez, CA
Assistant Director of Nutritional Services   12/06–Present

LONE TREE CONVALESCENT HOSPITAL, Antioch, CA
Dietary Supervisor   4/04–12/06

UNIVERSITY OF PITTSBURGH MEDICAL CENTER, Farrell, PA
Nutritional Services Team Leader   5/03–3/04
Dietetic Technician   9/99–5/03

EDUCATION

YOUNGSTOWN STATE UNIVERSITY, Youngstown, OH   9/01–3/02
Master of Science courses—Health and Human Services
Accounting and Science courses

INDIANA UNIVERSITY OF PENNSYLVANIA, Indiana, PA   1999
Bachelor of Science—Dietetics
Concentration—Hotel, Restaurant, and Institutional Management

LEADERSHIP

Safety Committee Chairman, Lone Tree Convalescent Hospital
Member, UPMC Horizon Quality Improvement Team

Figure 4.4: A sample combination resume.

Pick-Up Lines: Cover Letters

"Hi, my name is Right…Mr./Ms. Right." Although that would be a terrible pick-up line (maybe one of the worst ever), it's the right message for your cover letter. After all, you are trying to convince the employer that you are the right candidate for the job. Without a strong introduction, chances are you won't get very far with other singles. Without a strong cover letter, your resume won't get very far with recruiters.

I know what you're thinking: Nobody reads cover letters, and all of my important information is already in my resume. In some cases you might be right. Two recruiters from two different Fortune 500 companies recently told me that, due to the high volume of e-mails they receive from applicants, they don't read cover letters (or thank-you letters, for that matter). To them, your cover letter can only hurt your chances of getting an interview, not help them. Listing the wrong company name or having a bunch of typos is your ticket straight to Rejectionville, USA, population you.

However, I've also worked with recruiters who have gone over cover letters with a fine-toothed comb. Anytime you're submitting a cover letter, and you almost always will be, there's a very good chance someone will read it, or at least scan it. I recently spoke to just such a recruiter; she pointed out that every cover letter she received was very well written.

Even if an employer says a cover letter is optional, including one with your resume is still a good idea because it contains important information on the position you're applying for (title, where you saw the position posted, and so on) and something as simple as who your application should be delivered to at the company.

Together, your resume and cover letter present the argument that you are the candidate who should be hired. The cover letter, your introduction to the recruiter, provides you with an opportunity to make that argument in plain language, whereas the resume is necessarily a less graceful version of that compelling argument.

As outlined by the cover letter template shown in figure 4.5, every cover letter has three critical components: your introductory paragraph, the body of your letter, and your closing paragraph. The following sections give more details on each of these, as well as the format and the salutation.

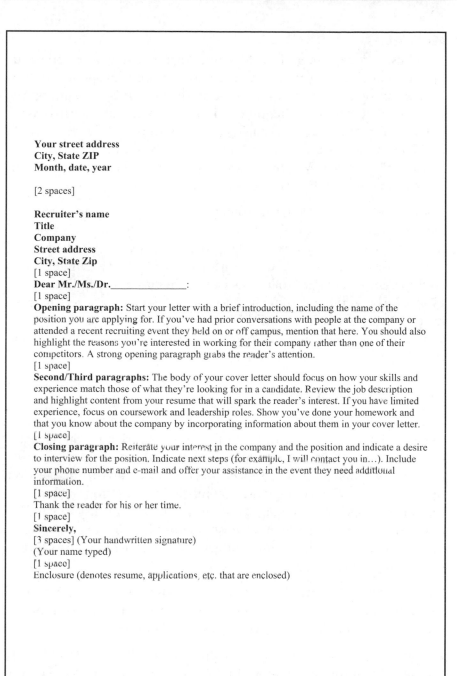

Your street address
City, State ZIP
Month, date, year

[2 spaces]

Recruiter's name
Title
Company
Street address
City, State Zip
[1 space]
Dear Mr./Ms./Dr._____:
[1 space]
Opening paragraph: Start your letter with a brief introduction, including the name of the position you are applying for. If you've had prior conversations with people at the company or attended a recent recruiting event they held on or off campus, mention that here. You should also highlight the reasons you're interested in working for their company rather than one of their competitors. A strong opening paragraph grabs the reader's attention.
[1 space]
Second/Third paragraphs: The body of your cover letter should focus on how your skills and experience match those of what they're looking for in a candidate. Review the job description and highlight content from your resume that will spark the reader's interest. If you have limited experience, focus on coursework and leadership roles. Show you've done your homework and that you know about the company by incorporating information about them in your cover letter.
[1 space]
Closing paragraph: Reiterate your interest in the company and the position and indicate a desire to interview for the position. Indicate next steps (for example, I will contact you in...). Include your phone number and e-mail and offer your assistance in the event they need additional information.
[1 space]
Thank the reader for his or her time.
[1 space]
Sincerely,
[3 spaces] (Your handwritten signature)
(Your name typed)
[1 space]
Enclosure (denotes resume, applications, etc. that are enclosed)

Figure 4.5: Cover letter template.

Salutation

Avoid using "Dear Sir and/or Madam," or other similar generic salutations, if at all possible. Finding the name of the appropriate contact person can be difficult, but try to locate the person by looking on the company Web site or in the job description. Then address the cover letter to him or her. If all else fails, it is okay to use "Dear Recruiter" or "To Whom It May Concern." However, it's not okay to use "Dear Sir" or "Dear Madam" because you never know the gender of the person who will be reading your letter.

If you're addressing a letter to someone and you're unsure as to whether that person is male or female because of the spelling of his or her name, try to verify this by calling the company. Or if you're unsure of the person's sex, do not list Mr. or Ms. For example, you could write, "Dear Pat Hollis" instead of the more usual, "Dear Ms. Hollis." This is the only time it is acceptable to address a recruiter by his or her first name in a formal letter. I've seen more than one person assume that Kelli with an "i" is a woman and address the person as Ms. only to find out Kelli is a man.

Introductory Paragraph

A strong introductory paragraph is like a great ice breaker with someone you'd like to ask out. Instead of mentioning friends you have in common, you can mention people you know who work at the company. For example, if you've spoken with someone about the position or you've had a chance to attend a company presentation, include that in your opening paragraph. One word of caution: If you were referred by someone and you plan on mentioning that person's name in your cover letter, make sure you get his or her permission before you do any name-dropping.

You'll also want to include the title of the position you're applying for and where you saw the posting or heard about the job (campus career center, company Web site, newspaper, and so on).

I review a lot of cover letters that include useless fluff such as "Attached you will find a copy of my resume, which details my educational background and work experience." Sentences like this add no value to the cover letter. Resumes provide details of your educational background and work experience by definition. Instead, say something like "I have attached a copy of my resume for your reference." Figure 4.6 provides a sample.

Body

The body of your cover letter should focus on your accomplishments. To customize your cover letter, take a close look at the job description and use the skills it lists to bolster your argument that you are the right person for this job. Once you know what the employer wants in a candidate, you can highlight examples from your background that match those needs.

The body focuses on some combination of academic background and work experience. If your resume is light on experience, pull in examples from school that illustrate your ability to do the job you are applying for. They can include projects, leadership roles, relevant coursework, and so on. On the flip side, if you didn't attend or finish college, or you've been out of college for several years, focus on your experience and how that lends itself to the position.

Closing Paragraph

The closing paragraph is important, but it doesn't require the pizzazz of the introductory paragraph. It gives you a chance to express your interest in the position one last time and to let the employer know you'll be following up to discuss the possibility of scheduling an interview. It's always a good idea to include your phone number and e-mail address again in case your resume and cover letter get separated.

Before sending your cover letter, be sure to sign your name at the bottom. If you're sending it via e-mail, you can either type your name in the same font as the rest of your letter or scan your signature and insert it electronically.

In addition to the components I've just discussed, format and salutation are also important parts of any cover letter. Take a look at some guidelines and advice for each in the following sections.

1 River Crossing Drive
Chapel Hill, NC 27517
(Date)

Mr. Phillip Jones
Institutional Sales, Equities Division
Acme Securities
100 East 14th Street
New York, NY 10004

Dear Mr. Jones:

I am writing to express my interest in interviewing for a position in Equity Research. I was highly impressed with Acme Securities' presentations to Big State University this fall. I also enjoyed meeting with your colleagues when I visited New York City in November.

I am familiar with Acme Securities' excellent reputation and consistently strong ranking in Equity Research. Also, lead managing 14 successful initial public offerings this year is evidence of your firm's strong culture and ability to succeed during difficult economic conditions. This has heightened my desire to work for Acme Securities.

Over the last five years, I have worked in financial institution mergers and acquisitions. Some of my accomplishments during this period include receiving the CFA designation, creating an equity research product for thinly traded banks, and managing multiple bank and thrift transactions. While pursuing my MBA, I continue to be employed as an independent financial consultant. I have worked hard over this period to develop my skills in anticipation of pursuing an Equity Research position following graduate school.

I have enclosed a copy of my resume for your review. If you have any further questions regarding my qualifications, please do not hesitate to contact me at 919-555-5555.

Thank you for your time and consideration.

Respectfully,

Alex Applicant

Alex Applicant, CFA

Enclosure

Figure 4.6: A sample cover letter.

Format

Cover letters are usually four to five paragraphs long and should be no longer than one page. Margins on the letter should be evenly spaced—typically 1 inch. Font size should fall between 10.5 and 12 points, and although it doesn't necessarily have to be the same size as the font you use on your resume, it should be close and should definitely be in the same font. Don't use Garamond font on your cover letter and Comic Sans font on your resume; they are part of a total package, and you want them to be consistent. If you decide to use colored resume paper (light gray or cream are your two best choices), the paper you use for your cover letter should match it.

TIP: As with resumes, having as many sets of eyes as possible proofread your cover letter for typos and other errors is essential.

I Want You to Want Me: How to Stand Out from Other Candidates

Let's travel back in time to the sixth grade, when love notes were all the rage. Remember those days? How would you feel if you were given a note that was made out to someone else or addressed "To whom it may concern?" If you are cutting corners while trying to make your best first impression, most employers will wonder what you will do if you get the job.

I know how tempting it can be to try a timesaving strategy, but don't send out the same cover letter over and over again, changing only the company name. A recruiter will notice the lack of effort. Although it's time-consuming, you need to customize each and every job application so that it is carefully aimed at the unique combination of skills and experience that each job requires. More importantly, a custom cover letter conveys an intangible—and vital—sense that you are enthusiastic about the company and about the job. Someone's far more likely to interview you if he or she thinks you're likely to successfully make it through the interview process.

Don't panic. Typically, I'm not talking about totally rewriting your entire resume and cover letter. Rather, I'm talking about going back over both documents to flesh out the skills and abilities the company desires. Look at the job description. Determine the key traits the organization is looking for in a candidate. If the number-one thing the organization is looking for is someone with prior supervisory experience and you list that as one of the last bullets on your resume, consider moving the bullet to the top. The same holds true with your cover letter. It's not enough to repeat your resume in paragraph form. Point out key highlights from your experience and link those highlights to the job you're applying for. By doing so, you'll have a much better chance at making the cut than those who cut and paste their way through the job search.

Follow up with the company after you've submitted your resume. In a recent survey conducted by staffing firm Robert Half International, 82 percent of executives polled said applicants should follow up with hiring managers within two weeks of submitting application materials.[2] Following up can literally bring your application to the top of the pile of the hundreds of other applications the company has received. It also shows the hiring company that you have drive and initiative.

Making Your Move: Submitting Your Resume and Cover Letter

When you're interested in someone, there are many ways to make your move. You can offer to buy that person a drink, give a seductive look from across a crowded room, or make no move at all (if your move is playing hard-to-get). During your job search, there are also many ways to make your move. The following sections give tips on the most common and effective ways.

Applying via E-mail

Often, a company may ask you to e-mail your cover letter and resume. In most cases, you'll be asked to attach your resume and cover letter to an e-mail as one Word document. After you combine

---

2. Robert Half International. "Don't Be a Stranger." www.roberthalffinance.com/ PressRoom?LOBName=RH&releaseid=1604. Accessed 27 October 2006.

your resume and cover letter into one file, save your document as a name that the recruiter will associate with you. Typically, *lastname-firstname.doc* works fine.

If you're attaching your resume and cover letter to the e-mail, you should include a brief introductory message indicating that your resume and cover letter are attached. You don't need to include your entire cover letter in this brief introduction, but you do need to let the reader know why you are writing while hitting some of the key highlights from your background that you think will make the reader want to review your attached resume and cover letter. Compare the content of the sample e-mail in figure 4.7 with the content of the more traditional cover letters covered earlier in this chapter. Notice that both have strong opening paragraphs and provide key highlights from the applicant's background. However, because you are most likely going to attach a copy of your cover letter in its entirety, your e-mail will be much more concise than a traditional cover letter.

```
Dear Mr. Jones:

The attached resume and cover letter are submitted
in response to the position currently available at
HealthWise Services. I have spoken to a number of your
colleagues, including Jim Jenkins and Vicki Jones,
about applying for this position and I am enthusiastic
about the opportunity to join a cutting-edge healthcare firm.

I believe my undergraduate degree in healthcare policy
at UCLA, coupled with my prior experience at Blue Cross/
Blue Shield, will enable me to make a strong positive
contribution to the company.

I look forward to speaking with you about the opening.
Please let me know if you would like me to send my resume
and cover letter in a different format.

Thank you for your time and consideration.

Best,
Robert Student
```

Figure 4.7: An e-mail cover letter.

Limiting the length of your e-mail can also have its benefits. Recruiters typically go through their in-boxes pretty quickly due to the high volume of e-mails they receive daily. They don't want to spend a lot of time reading through each and every e-mail. The more concise and compelling you are in your e-mail, the better your chances of getting noticed.

To avoid potential formatting quirks that may arise if an employer opens your resume with a different version of the software you used to create it, consider converting your resume to an Adobe Portable Document Format (PDF) file.

Applying at the Company Web Site

More and more companies are asking candidates to apply for open positions through their Web sites. The application process can vary greatly, but it typically involves a combination of filling out an online form and pasting or attaching your resume. When you paste your resume on a company Web site, almost all your formatting is lost. Luckily, most company Web sites provide specific instructions on how to submit your resume electronically; make sure you read their guidelines carefully. To convert your resume to an Internet-compatible, plain text format, follow these steps:

1. Save your Word document as a "Text Only (*.txt)" document.

2. Open the .txt file and adjust formatting so that information is easy to find and read.

3. Use a plain font such as Arial or Times New Roman.

4. Left-justify all text, including category headings. Change all bullets to dashes or asterisks.

When your reformatting is complete, you'll be able to cut and paste all or part of your resume into online job applications.

Applying Through the Mail

If you're mailing a hard copy of your resume and cover letter, there are a few things to keep in mind. Be sure to check the print quality of your documents. Laser printers can run out of toner, and the ink from an ink-jet printer can smear or print unevenly. As mentioned in the cover letter section, if you decide to print your resume and cover letter on colored paper, be sure you use the same colored paper for both; after all, they're part of a package. I recommend buying 9 × 12 white envelopes. That way, you can avoid folding your resume and cover letter, thus making it easier for the person trying to read or make copies of them. You can then print white or clear mailing labels, and you'll end up with a nice, clean package.

NOTE: You might be thinking that your envelope doesn't matter, but I've heard of a number of organizations that forward your envelope to hiring managers along with your resume and cover letter.

Just the Fax

Every so often, a company will ask you to fax your application materials. The key point to remember is to create a cover sheet. Different from a cover letter, a cover sheet indicates who sent the fax, when it was sent, what it's about, and who should receive the fax. The cover sheet can also help keep the content of your cover letter and resume somewhat confidential. Microsoft Word offers a number of fax cover sheet templates that you can customize. Don't worry about printing your resume and cover letter on fancy paper; plain white will do just fine. Resume paper with a lot of texture will probably only decrease the quality of your fax.

Chapter 5

Finding Mr. or Ms. Right: Job Search Resources

"With the rise of the Internet, more people are using search engines and databases to find both job and relationship prospects, but many people still rely on the more old-fashioned word of mouth."

—Jenna, job seeker

Some people are proactive, aggressively looking for Mr. or Ms. Right, while others sit back and wait for opportunity to knock. If you're attracted to Domino's or Papa John's delivery drivers, then maybe the sitting-around approach works for you. I don't know about you, but I've had some pretty strange people knock on my door over the past few years. Just last month, a guy knocked on my door at 9 p.m. and wanted to know if I needed an oil change. If that was opportunity knocking, I wasn't answering.

When it comes to your job search, being proactive is the only way to go. Before continuing, I want to clarify that being proactive does not mean calling the CEO of a Fortune 500 company and asking whether he or she knows of any job openings at that particular organization. That approach might work, but more often than not it will ruin your chances with that company.

How can you be proactive in your job search? Search for opportunities that aren't posted on the Web or in your local newspaper. Talk to friends, classmates, professors, and family. Share your interests and the types of positions you're looking for. At this stage of the game, you're going to have to kiss a lot of frogs before you find your prince or princess. The more you pucker up, the more you'll be able to uncover those hard-to-find job opportunities.

A number of resources are available to assist you in locating job openings, and this chapter looks at the advantages and disadvantages of each. Based on what you're looking for, you'll need to decide what combination of resources you'll use. Don't hurt your chances of finding a job by using only one or two job search resources; flexibility early in the process can be very beneficial. As you continue your search, you'll have time to determine which job search resources produce more and better leads than others, and you'll be able to start narrowing your focus to specific companies and geographic areas.

Now that I've set the stage, take a look at the resources that can help you find Mr. or Ms. Right, or in this case, your dream job. I've organized them in order of importance, with networking coming first and executive search firms last.

Matchmakers: Networking

If you're single, sometimes your friends play matchmaker and try to hook you up with some of their single friends. Without these matchmakers, you might not get a chance to meet the people they're trying to connect you with. During your job search, networking can be a lot like matchmaking. People you meet will often try to connect you with people looking to hire qualified candidates.

When you were just gathering information about various careers and trying to narrow down your interests, you most likely talked to a number of people at different companies. Some of them were probably very helpful, whereas others tried to avoid you like the plague. Think back to your conversations. Is there anyone who might be able to assist you in locating job openings in a certain industry or with a certain company? If the answer is no, don't be afraid to contact more people. If the answer is yes, reach out and give that person an update on how your job search has been going since you last connected. For example, if you spoke with someone over the summer but haven't been in touch since you returned to school, you might start an e-mail to that person by mentioning that you're back on campus. Then you could transition into coursework, your internship, or your job search, depending on your situation.

Meeting New People

As I mentioned in chapter 3, possible networking contacts can be sitting next to you on a plane or standing beside you in line at the grocery store. I once counseled a 28-year-old client interested in making a career change to pharmaceutical sales in Erie, Pennsylvania. I suggested she talk to people she ran into during her day-to-day activities, and guess what? During a flight, she happened to sit next to a pharmaceutical sales representative who worked in Erie. The person was more than willing to tell her about the industry, but she didn't offer her business card as they got off the plane. The client could have asked for one, but she didn't; so she wasn't able to expand her job search network. On the bright side, she was able to gather information that helped her prepare for interviews and ultimately secure a job with another company.

When I graduated from college, I didn't have a job lined up or any networking contacts. I submitted applications to a number of local companies and ended up grabbing the first offer that came along. Unfortunately, after two years on the job, I was downsized. When that happened, I was shell-shocked. I had limited experience, and I wasn't sure which way to turn. What can I say? Sometimes getting dumped can really suck. I knew I didn't want to go back into retail, but because that's where my experience was, those were the only positions companies wanted to interview me for. One thing I had thought about, because I spent so much time on my job search when I was an undergrad, was working for a college or university in a career-services office. The only problem was that I didn't have any connections.

I decided to continue actively looking for job opportunities in different industries while also contacting local colleges and universities and offering to work free as an intern. I ended up sending my resume and cover letter to three schools. How many do you think I heard from? One. Talk about a blow to my self-esteem when I was already on the rebound. As it turns out, it was the best thing that could have happened to me. The school I heard from brought me on as an intern, and I was fortunate enough to be hired for a full-time position shortly thereafter. In my case, I didn't have an established network to help me transition into a new career field, so I had to create one from scratch.

As I continue to play the field and meet new people, I've been able to learn about a number of openings before they were even posted. This is a great situation to be in; my chances of securing an interview for positions that haven't been posted place me pretty far ahead of the hundreds of applicants applying for jobs online or listed in the newspaper. If I hear about something that others don't know about yet, I already have an advantage. Even if the opening is posted, I have the chance to apply early and make a contact that will help me stand out.

Keep in Touch!

Even after you've found your dream job, be sure to stay in touch with the people in your network. Send them an occasional e-mail message. Let them know where you're working. Most people fall out of touch with professional contacts after they've found the job they were looking for, but it's important to remember that networking is a lifelong process. You never know when you might need a job, or when someone from your network might offer you a spectacular opportunity. So it's important that you work hard to maintain and expand your network; it will play a vital role in your success throughout your career.

TIP: Effective networking requires spending a considerable amount of time getting to know people. The focus is on the quality of your interactions with different contacts, not necessarily the number of people you speak with.

Clubbing: Career Fairs

Think of career fairs as clubbing for job seekers. They offer a great way to make contact with a large number of employers in a short period of time. They also allow you to practice your job search and conversational skills.

Preparing for a Career Fair

Most career fairs supply you with a list of companies whose representatives will be attending before the actual event takes place. This information, if available, gives you a chance to research each organization, including its products, services, culture, and competitors. You can also find out ahead of time which positions each organization is looking to fill. That way, you can develop a strategy—a case for why the company should hire you instead of anyone else. Then, when you talk to a representative at the fair, you can ask educated questions about the position, company, and industry. Sample questions can include the following:

- What is a typical career path for a college graduate starting in an entry-level position with your organization?

- What skills are most important for an entry-level candidate to possess?

- What kinds of career opportunities are available for my degree and skills?

- What are some typical first-year assignments?

- What personality traits are important for success within your organization?

- Does your organization like to promote from within?

In this sense, preparing for a career fair can be a lot like preparing for a date. Before the date, you can't envision yourself making conversation with a stranger. But you definitely need to consider the conversation topics that might be most effective in making small talk during your date.

Five Tips for Working a Career Fair

1. Determine target organizations.
2. Don't monopolize a recruiter's time.
3. Avoid taking a lot of free stuff.
4. Collect business cards.
5. Follow up with contacts after the fair.

Plan ahead. Identify and research companies you want to speak with at the fair (full-fledged interviews typically won't take place at the fair, but every once in a while they do). Knowing which companies you're interested in is also a great way to gauge how many copies of your resume you should bring. You don't want to run out, but you also don't need to make 400 copies for a fair with 35 employers.

Working the Room

One of your aims in attending a career fair should be to expand your base of networking contacts. Even though getting business cards from employer representatives at large fairs is sometimes difficult because recruiters don't want to get bombarded with phone calls and e-mails, it never hurts to ask.

TIP: Always dress professionally for career fairs; you can't go wrong with a conservative business suit and a nice pair of leather dress shoes. For specific guidelines on what to wear, refer to chapter 6.

When a recruiter doesn't give you his or her business card, don't give up. After the fair, check with your college or university career center to see whether that recruiter's contact information might already be on file. If it isn't, you still might be able to figure out that person's e-mail by looking at the way e-mail addresses are formatted for other contacts at the company. Regardless, if you want to differentiate yourself from other candidates, you'll still want to reference your meeting at the fair in the opening paragraph of your cover letter or e-mail.

Sample Script: Approaching a Recruiter at a Career Fair

You: "Good morning *[insert recruiter's name if he or she is wearing a name tag or you happen to know his or her name].*" "My name is Jane Applicant. I am very interested in a research position with ABC Labs."

Recruiter: "Hi, Jane. Why are you interested in working with ABC Labs?"

You: "ABC Labs *[insert two or three key points that show the recruiter you really did your homework on the company before the fair, including visiting its Web site].*"

The conversation will typically continue for another two or three minutes (pay attention to any nonverbal signals the recruiter may be giving off if you're starting to overstay your welcome, including repeatedly looking at his or her watch or breaking eye contact to look at other waiting students). Highlight your successes in and out of the classroom. Mention prior positive interactions with alumni working at the company and other details that will help you stand out from the hundreds of other candidates the recruiter has met with throughout the day.

Sample questions you might ask:

- How many candidates will you be hiring?
- What are the next steps following today's career fair?
- What locations are you hiring for?
- May I have your business card?

At the end of your conversation, if the recruiter hasn't asked for a copy of your resume, offer to provide one. Close by thanking the recruiter for his or her time.

If you're interested in two organizations whose booths are right next to each other, try not to go directly from one to the other. Visit other companies of interest that are situated in another area and then go back to the other table later. It's simple etiquette—similar to the decision not to put the moves on someone right after you've approached someone else at the same bar. Don't create any room for misinterpretation—and don't make yourself look clueless about such important things as corporate rivalries. Even such details as who is hiring and for what positions can be viewed as confidential company data.

The typical amount of time you have to talk to a company representative will be about two to three minutes and can often depend on how many people are waiting in line. To maximize your time, develop a brief introduction that highlights your interest in the organization as well as your skills and experience, and practice your delivery until you feel comfortable. Don't panic; you'll be talking about things you've done, so an introduction like this should come relatively naturally. Rehearse but be sure to avoid sounding like a recording. The last thing an employer wants to see is a candidate who looks like he or she is reading from cue cards or reciting lines in the third-grade school play. Think of it as another opportunity to use the "60-second conversation" you developed in chapter 3.

Take some time to take a break during the fair. This will allow you to refresh yourself and write down notes about organizations you're interested in while they are still fresh in your mind. If you wait until the end of the fair, you might forget specific details or ideas about your next move, such as searching for sales opportunities on a certain company's Web site.

If employers are giving away a ton of freebies at their tables (and they all do), don't take a lot of stuff. I know the pencils and hats can be very tempting, but grabbing a bunch of free pencils and notepads will most likely hurt your chances with that company because you'll look greedy and unprofessional. Plus, the last thing you want to be carrying around is a giant bag of goodies from table to table like some kind of unemployed trick-or-treater (see figure 5.1). This also applies to food and drinks at company presentations. I've seen college and graduate students arrive late and interrupt a speaker because they were in the hall meticulously arranging a plate of select fruit and cheese as though it were to appear on the *Food Network*. Whether you're at a career fair or a company-sponsored recruiting event, your objective is to get a job or internship, not to grab as much free stuff as you can. Moderation is the key. Focus too much on the free stuff, and that splendid-looking fruit and cheese plate might be the only thing you have to show for your efforts.

If you're unsure about how much free stuff you should consume, think about how you would handle the situation if you were on a date. Say you've decided to dine at a Mexican restaurant that offers complimentary chips with every meal. You wouldn't be very impressed with your

Figure 5.1: The unemployed trick-or-treater.

date if he or she tore through three or four helpings before the meal even arrived. And while we're on the topic of food, if possible, try to avoid eating anything at a career fair. You could accidentally spill something on yourself, or you could even end up talking to recruiters the rest of the afternoon without knowing you had some food stuck in your teeth the whole time.

Finding Career Fairs

Some career fairs are open to the general public, whereas others aren't. For example, most colleges and universities hold annual fairs that are open only to students currently enrolled at their institution or those who have recently graduated. If you have any doubts as to whether you're allowed to participate, call for details (especially when you're planning to travel to the fair from out of town). If you're considering relocating to a different state and are planning to attend a career fair in that area, find out whether there are any other upcoming fairs so that you can plan accordingly.

To find out about career fairs in your area, check with your campus career office and local newspaper and search online job-posting sites on a regular basis. Your local unemployment office should also be able to inform you of any upcoming career events in your area.

Career fairs allow you to connect with a large number of recruiters from different industries in a short period of time. And if you like large numbers of recruiters, then the next section is just for you. Coming up, we look at popular job search Web sites.

Online Dating: Popular Job Search Web Sites

Dozens of Web sites offer millions of job openings as well as personal listings from those looking for a mate. Newspapers and the Internet can be highly effective, but they shouldn't be your only strategy. Why? Relying solely on postings is a reactive strategy: You're reacting to what is placed in front of you. It's important to point out that these openings are posted to a very large target audience, and you could be one of hundreds, if not thousands, applying for one opening or trying to get one date.

> *Match.com = Monster.com without the clear compensation structure.*
>
> —Fred, job seeker

Disadvantages of Looking Online

In a perfect world, people would apply for only those positions for which they are qualified. Unfortunately, this isn't always the case. If a company is looking for someone with a Ph.D. in anthropology, 24 people with an associate's degree in hotel/restaurant management will apply. To them, the desire to find any job is more important than focusing on openings that they are genuinely interested in or qualified for. And that's in a *good* economy. Think about how that number rises when people really start getting desperate for work. You might be the most qualified person for the position, but sometimes you can get lost in the shuffle when your application is thrown in with so many others. In response, many companies are starting to limit advertisements of available jobs on job boards so that they don't have to deal with the thousands of e-mails that come in from any one listing. They are instead often relying on referrals and networking to fill open positions.

Another disadvantage of online job databases involves third-party recruiters who often list positions online on behalf of the employer.

These postings can make it difficult or next to impossible to tell who the actual hiring company is or for you to follow up after you've applied for the opening. I'm sure you've seen ads in the "Help Wanted" section that don't list the name of the organization but rather list a P.O. box or a toll-free phone number. I once applied for a consulting position that was advertised like that. When I received a call from a headhunter a few days later, I wasn't sure why she was calling until she told me the consulting position I'd applied for didn't actually exist. The staffing agency had run the ad because it was looking for someone to join its firm who possessed the qualifications and skills that were listed in the advertisement. I told the headhunter I didn't appreciate the way the agency conducted its search. I also said I wasn't interested in working with the agency. To me, this situation was the equivalent of meeting someone in a chat room, only to find out the person you thought was Carla is actually a 450-pound shut-in named Carl with a six-month free trial of AOL. Somebody call Jerry Springer!

On the Plus Side...

Online databases do have their advantages. First and foremost, they allow you to access job openings from around the world, 24 hours a day, 7 days a week. Some services allow you to post your resume online and also send you e-mail notifications when new positions matching your interests have been posted. Monster, CareerBuilder, Yahoo! HotJobs, Craigslist, and Jobs.com are examples of large, general job-posting sites. Most of these sites contain positions for all ranges of experience, from entry-level to seasoned professional, and offer the ability to search for positions by industry and career level. They also offer resume-writing advice and other tools that can assist you with your job search.

See table 5.1 for some additional benefits and downsides to this approach.

Table 5.1: Pros and Cons of Using the Web in Your Job Search

Pros	Cons
Access to job-posting sites containing thousands of openings from around the world	Competition from hundreds, if not thousands, of applicants
Applying directly to companies accepting online applications through their Web sites	Trying to find an actual person you can speak with at the company about job openings
Searching large amounts of information to conduct company and industry research	Potential for information overload
Posting your resume online	Potential privacy issues

Niche Sites and Other More Focused Places to Look

A number of Web sites focus on jobs and internships in specific industries and functions. Check the appendix for examples. If you are focusing on a particular industry, these sites can be very effective. Companies looking for someone with a very specific background often use these sites first to locate talent.

Similar openings can also be found on professional association Web sites. If you aren't sure of the professional associations or industry-specific posting sites that are available, try searching online for the keywords "professional associations" and the industry you're interested in or refer to the *Encyclopedia of Associations.*

Newspapers from most large cities are now also available online and can prove to be a great resource if you're looking for positions in a specific geographic region. If you're considering a job in another state, locate the appropriate newspaper for that area and see whether a classified ads section is available online. Some newspapers charge a subscription fee for you to access their paper, so check around to see what's available for free before writing any checks.

Online databases and classified ads are great resources for uncovering job opportunities in your geographic area and around the world. The same holds true for company Web sites, which provide an added benefit: They allow you to apply directly to companies of interest. The next section includes advice on how to find jobs on company Web sites.

Personal Ads: Company Web Sites

We've all seen personal ads listed in the local newspaper. When you want to find that special someone, you might run a similar ad or log onto dating sites like eHarmony, Match.com, or Yahoo! Personals. When companies want to find that special someone, they post their openings on job search sites such as Monster, and they also post openings on their company Web sites. Every site is a little bit different, but you should be on the lookout for a "Jobs" or "Careers" link somewhere on the home page. If you don't see the link, look under "About Us" or a similar page. When you find the right page, you should be able to search available positions by location and job function.

> **ARE YOU OUT THERE?**
>
> Single athletic female seeks single athletic male who enjoys long walks on the beach, dancing, movies, and having fun. ☎ 5765

As mentioned earlier, be sure to print descriptions of jobs you're interested in applying for because they are often removed from the Web site without notice. Having the descriptions will assist you in keeping track of positions you are applying for and will also help you prepare for interviews. Plus, there's nothing worse than getting a call from an employer wanting to schedule an interview and not recalling the name of the job or the description of the position you'll be interviewing for. The last thing you want to do is to have to ask someone to send you the description again because it makes you look disorganized and scattered.

> **ARE YOU OUT THERE?**
>
> 35 YO LMC seeking intelligent overachiever interested in a possible long-term relationship. ☎ 2323

ABBREVIATIONS: Year-Old; Large Multinational Corporation

Knowing how to effectively use the Web during your job search is going to save you time and increase your chances of getting an interview with companies of interest. But without someone in the company pulling for you, your application might get lost among the thousands of others received. Networking is not only a great way to make sure you stand out from the crowd after you've applied for jobs and internships online, but also a great way for you to find out about opportunities before they even are posted.

Depending on your level of success in finding a full-time job through networking, career fairs, and the Web, you might be curious about reaching out to an executive search firm. The next section includes information on when you might consider these services and what you should look out for.

Personal Matchmaking Services: Executive and Other Search Firms

During a recent flight to New York, I decided to pass the time by reading the "award-winning" complimentary in-flight magazine. As I skimmed the magazine, I noticed an ad for a personal matchmaking service that was started by a former executive recruiter. That, and the fact that I had nothing else to do besides wait for my tiny bag of complimentary pretzels and refreshing soda, gave me time to think about how similar dating services and executive search firms really are. Personal matchmakers and executive search firms are both trying to do the same thing—link singles to other singles, or in this case, candidates to companies.

If you're looking for middle- or upper-management executive positions, or you're just not having luck uncovering jobs of interest, a search firm might be for you. If you think you need professional assistance with your search and don't know where to look for firms in your area, start with the Yellow Pages under the heading "Employment Agencies." You'll notice generalist firms and those that focus their services on specific industries and experience levels. It's important to pick a firm that is familiar with your area of interest because it'll most likely have established relationships and a track record of placing people with the organizations you are considering.

Before committing to a specific recruiting organization, call different firms and ask questions about what services are offered. Some will require you to go through a screening interview with them before they agree to work with you. Treat the screening interview seriously.

Be ready to talk about your skills and be sure to dress professionally; the recruiting firm will be evaluating your marketability and professionalism as it decides whether to work with you and how much of its valuable time you deserve. Another reason the screening interview is important is that staffing agencies make more or less money on you based purely on your marketability as a job candidate. Try to impress your interviewers or even make friends with them, and they'll likely work much harder to place you in an excellent job.

Once you've selected a recruitment firm, be sure you understand any and all agreements you are asked to sign. The salary, for example, may not be what it seems if the agency plans to extract a fee from it. If you have any doubts about the firm or the contract, don't feel obligated to sign anything on the spot. Reputable firms will allow you to take some time to think about your decision.

Executive search firms often charge fees for their services. These fees are paid either by the employer looking to hire someone, or by you, the client. If you aren't sure about the fee structure and whether you're responsible for paying, ask directly. The last thing you want to do is unwittingly sign a contract stating you're responsible for paying some portion of your first year's salary that could be as much as 10 to 15 percent. And if the hiring company is responsible for paying the fee, is the contract structured such that it provides both the company and the staffing agency incentives for treating you well?

Some large organizations rely exclusively on third-party recruiters to address their hiring needs. If you're interested in working for a particular company that uses an outside source for recruiting, find out which firm it uses and contact that firm directly. This can be a great way to get your foot in the door. Even if you're hired for a short-term or part-time assignment, you might have opportunities to network with people within the organization. Limited-term contract or temporary work can also provide an opportunity to prove to the company that you're able to do the job, hugely increasing your chances of being hired for a permanent position at a later date. Of course, not all temporary assignments lead to long-term positions, but they are something to consider.

Networking, career fairs, the Web, and executive search firms can all be great resources for locating internships and jobs. Now that you've seen the pros and cons of each and how they might fit into your job search strategy, I'll focus on how you can stand out from your competition by reaching out to companies after you've applied for openings.

I'll Give You a Call Sometime: Following Up with Companies After You've Applied for an Opening

Just as important as calling someone you'd like to ask out after you've exchanged phone numbers, following up with a company where you've applied for a job is usually a good idea. It not only shows your ability to take the initiative and your enthusiasm about the job, but can also help differentiate you from others who didn't take the time to send a quick e-mail or make a telephone call. Follow-up is best when you identify and call the department doing the hiring, not just human resources. The reason is that the department heads are going to be the ones working with human resources to determine who gets an interview and who doesn't.

Fight the Post-Interview Jitters

Reaching out to a company about a job opening you're interested in can be a scary and awkward part of the application process. It can be as nerve-wracking (if not more so) as calling someone you just met to see whether he or she would like to go out on a date with you. Part of the reason it's so awkward is that you don't know what's going to happen or how the person is going to react. When it comes to following up on a job application, it's hard sometimes to know whom to call, what to say, or even how long you should wait before calling. However, there are a few things you can do to make following up a little bit easier. First, think through what you're going to say. The main objectives of your follow-up phone call will be to

- See what the next steps of the interview process are.

- Inquire about a possible time frame when interviews will take place.

- Show the employer your ability to take the initiative, which can help differentiate you from other candidates.

Next, rehearse the conversation. The more comfortable you become with what you're going to say, the more confident you'll be when you call. Then, take a few deep breaths. Finally, when you feel ready, make the call.

Although there are no actual rules about how many days you should wait between applying for a position and calling the company, waiting five business days should give the company enough time to process your application. But depending on how many applicants are being considered, the length of time needed to process your application could vary considerably.

When Not to Call

Even though I've stressed the importance of following up your application with a phone call, in some cases, you shouldn't do so. For example, if the company specifies "no phone calls, please" in its ad or on its Web site, that's a good indication that you shouldn't call. Although the follow-up phone call can serve to show that you're serious about the job, if the company has directed you not to call, doing so could negatively impact your candidacy by showing that you're unable to follow directions.

TIP: Just as important as calling someone you'd like to ask out after you've exchanged phone numbers, following up with a company where you've applied for a job is a must.

Pull an Inside Job

In every case, it is to your advantage to locate someone within the company with whom you have or can develop a rapport. That way, you have a person on the inside who can help your chances by making sure your application gets in front of the right people. It's like befriending the friends of someone you'd like to date—if they like you, you're in.

In the case of the follow-up phone call, your networking efforts will really pay off if the insider you've developed a relationship with can tell you whom to call and how to approach this person about the job you've applied for.

The biggest drawback of applying for positions online is how difficult it is to follow up and see whether you're being considered. Online job postings often don't list a contact person. It's possible you'll receive an automatic response stating that your application has been received, but trying to speak with someone about it, usually someone in human resources who won't be working with you if you're eventually hired, can be very difficult. But that doesn't mean you shouldn't try. If you are able to find a general telephone number on the company's site, or better yet, a contact name and number in human resources, you should call to follow up after submitting your materials online.

The Three-Day Rule

After you decide to call to follow up on your job application, remember that certain times of the day work better than others. Relatively early in the morning, over lunch, or late in the afternoon are good times to try to reach someone at your target organization. But bear in mind that first thing Monday morning or 5 p.m. on Friday are not good times to call because people are either swamped on their first day back in the office or tying up loose ends before leaving for the weekend.

What to Say

When you're able to get someone on the phone, introduce yourself and state why you're calling. Mentioning the position you applied for will help avoid any confusion. You should be able to tell pretty quickly whether that person is interested in talking to you. If he or she responds with short answers or sounds annoyed, thank your contact person for his or her time and try to end the call as soon as possible. Don't hurt your chances by getting on the wrong side of someone in human resources, or even someone you'll one day be working with. Here is a sample cold-calling script for following up after applying for a job or internship opening.

Sample Script: Calling to Follow Up After Applying for an Opening

"Good morning or afternoon [insert his or her name]."

"I recently applied for the [insert job title] position, and I wanted to call and check the status of my application. I also wanted to inquire about next steps and a possible time frame for the interview process."

Roadblock

"We haven't made any decisions yet."

Possible Response

"Thanks for the update. Can you give me an idea of when you think decisions will be made?"

Roadblock

"The job has been filled."

Possible Response

"I am still very much interested in working for [insert company name]. Would it be possible for me to contact you again in a few weeks to see whether any new opportunities have become available?"

If you're speaking with someone in human resources, it's important that you understand his or her role and how that person can assist you. In most cases, those working in HR are focused on the hiring process. They can tell you what you need to do to apply as well as answer questions about the number of positions they're looking to fill and an estimated time frame, if they have one. They may not have a say in the ultimate decision on whom to hire.

Think of HR staff as gatekeepers: They ultimately control whether your application gets into the right hands. It's like calling to speak with someone you're dating but finding that person isn't home, and speaking instead with his or her roommate. You'd better be nice to the roommate, or there's no guarantee the person you're calling will ever get your message. And you also should understand that people working in human resources are very busy, and that they often get bombarded with calls from job applicants. Therefore, you should make sure you've thought out your questions before you call and then be friendly and to-the-point.

If you're lucky enough to talk to the person who might be your boss if you're hired, the best way to make a good first impression is to articulate why you're interested in that particular position with the company. And if you can work it in, mention why you believe you'll be a good fit for that opening, based on your background. This is your chance to briefly highlight one or two of your strengths. Break out your "60-second conversation" from chapter 3. You don't have to brag, and you don't have to blurt out a 30-second autobiography without taking a breath, but you should be able to show a genuine interest in the position and an understanding of how you would fill that opening.

Guys'/Girls' Night Out: Taking a Break

When you're on the dating scene, sometimes you don't get to spend as much time with your friends as you did when you were single. After a while, you need to take a break for a guys'/girls' night out. When you take a break during your job search, it gives you a chance to evaluate your current job search strategy. How would you say you're doing so far? Are things going well? Are you having limited success? Is there anything you would like to do differently? Let's say you've applied to 10 different positions and didn't get any interviews. Before reinventing the wheel, take some time to evaluate any feedback you've received from companies or staffing agencies. Usually, you'll be lucky to get a rejection letter from companies you've applied to, so don't expect many employers to be forthcoming with constructive criticism on your application. It's nothing personal; they just get swamped with resumes and cover letters and don't have time to follow up with everyone.

If you possess the required qualifications and haven't been selected for an interview, go back and take a look at your resume and cover letter. Check for any typos, make sure your resume accurately reflects your experience, and have one of your friends read it to determine whether your cover letter is well written and concise.

Chapter 6

What Are You Going to Wear?: Dressing for Interview Success

"I think you should always want to look your best on a first date, because how you come across on that first date could very well determine if you get a second date. Similarly, when interviewing for a job, you want to show the interviewer that you mean business and are a professional, and that you care about yourself. If you don't appear to care about yourself, why would anyone think you cared about a job?"

—Kara, job seeker

Picking out the right outfit is one of the biggest things people worry most about before a date. They don't want to be under- or overdressed; and above all else, they want to look their best. When you're looking for a job, the outfit you pick is equally important.

Although there has been much debate in offices across the country about appropriate dress on the job, in the case of a job *interview,* it's always a good idea to dress as professionally as your budget allows. You don't have to buy a pricey designer suit, but you should have at least one conservative business suit to wear to an interview.

Four Items You Can Wear on a Date but Can't Wear on a Job Interview

1. Tank tops
2. Flip-flops
3. Baseball caps
4. Jeans

If you're worried about being overdressed for an interview at a company you know has a relaxed dress code, stop and consider the situation. The person interviewing you *has* the job and can wear flip-flops and khaki shorts—but you can't. During your interview, your appearance and behavior should project a certain degree of humility and respect. The only time you could ever overdress for an interview is if you wore a tuxedo or an evening gown. From grocery bagger to executive, I've never heard anyone say he or she didn't get a job because of being overdressed for the interview. But I guarantee that many people miss out on jobs every day because they're underdressed. If you're worried about what to wear, don't be. Up next, we'll look at everything you need to know about how to dress to impress.

Great Places to Buy Ties

*   Lee Allison (www.leeallison.com)
*   Hermès (www.hermes.com)
*   Brooks Brothers (www.brooksbrothers.com)
*   Vineyard Vines (www.vineyardvines.com)
*   Thomas Pink (www.thomaspink.co.uk/)
*   Paul Stuart (www.paulstuart.com)

Cocktail Party: Business Dress

Formal dates require formal dress. If you're going to a cocktail party, you can't show up in jeans and a t-shirt. Similarly, you can't show up to a job interview underdressed and expect to be invited back. If you want to look your best, you can't go wrong by wearing a nice suit.

Suggestions for Men

I recommend a suit and tie for almost every interview. Two- or three-button suits in navy, black, and charcoal are the most versatile and preferred by most companies.

Shirts

Shirt color and tie design can also vary based on your individual preference, but I recommend sticking with something conservative that accents your suit instead of competing with it. For an example of what not to wear, look no further than a story that one of my career-counseling colleagues told me. A few years back, as the story goes, he witnessed a graduate student wearing a totally inappropriate beaded tie on a company visit. Where does one buy a beaded tie? I don't know—and I don't want to know.

A white dress shirt is best, but only if you wear a plain white t-shirt underneath. Nothing kills an interview faster than the silhouette of a man's upper torso peaking through a white dress shirt. You want to look dignified and give the impression that you respect the company and the interviewer enough to go to some trouble preparing for the interview. The interviewer is well aware that if you get the job, you'll be representing the company and contributing to its image.

TIP: Practicing proper grooming, using conservative amounts of cologne or aftershave (or none at all), and removing any visible piercings are also critical if you hope to be successful during the interview process. You want the interviewer to focus on your skills and qualifications during the interview, not the diamond stud you have in your nose.

Ties and Shoes

The four-in-hand is the most popular tie knot for interviews. Figure 6.1 outlines the steps for creating a four-in-hand knot. Other popular tie knots include the half and double Windsors. Regardless of the knot you choose, when it's finished, the tips of your necktie should be long enough to hit the top of your belt buckle.

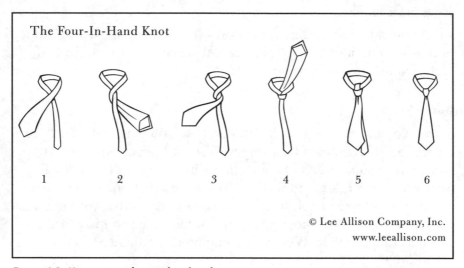

The Four-In-Hand Knot

1   2   3   4   5   6

© Lee Allison Company, Inc.
www.leeallison.com

Figure 6.1: How to tie a four-in-hand tie knot.

Be sure to have a pair of dress shoes that are in good shape and properly polished. As a general rule, the color of your shoes, your watchband, and your belt should always match. Black shoes can be worn with navy, charcoal, and black suits. Brown shoes can be worn with olive, brown, and taupe suits. Your sock color should complement your suit and not create a distraction. (Table 6.1 lists resources for suits.)

Table 6.1: Suit Yourself: Can't-Miss Buys for Any Budget

Men's Suits	Women's Suits
Zegna www.zegna.com	Ann Klein Available at Nordstrom
Hickey Freeman www.hickeyfreeman.com	Saks Fifth Avenue www.saksfifthavenue.com
Brooks Brothers www.brooksbrothers.com	Brooks Brothers www.brooksbrothers.com
Joseph A. Bank www.josbank.com	Nordstrom www.nordstrom.com
Banana Republic www.bananarepublic.com	Ann Taylor www.anntaylor.com
J. Crew www.jcrew.com	Banana Republic www.bananarepublic.com
Men's Wearhouse www.menswearhouse.com	J. Crew www.jcrew.com
S&K Men's Stores www.skmenswear.com	Dillard's www.dillards.com

Scale of 1 to 5, with 1 suit being inexpensive and 5 suits being expensive.

Suggestions for Women

A business suit is recommended for interviews. Although pants suits are more widely accepted today than they were 20 years ago, skirt suits are still preferred in conservative fields such as government, banking, or law. Similar to the color guidelines mentioned for men, suits for women will also vary by industry and company, but navy, black, and charcoal are the most widely accepted. Experts recommend that your skirt length fall at, or very close to, your knee. You should also be able to sit comfortably with your legs crossed without worrying about showing too much leg.

It's really hard to dress too conservatively for an interview. Here are some other tips for dressing for interview success:

- Closed-toed shoes are considered business professional. When you're wearing a business suit, a mid-height-heel classic pump with a minimal amount of decoration is most appropriate.

- Low-cut blouses, sleeveless tops, and sleeveless dresses are not acceptable.

- Some women may be extremely resistant to wearing pantyhose (and for good reason, my editor adds), but they're absolutely required at a job interview.

- Don't over-bling. Your jewelry should complement your appearance, not be a distraction.

- Your interviewer shouldn't be able to hear or smell you coming down the hall.

- Go easy on the makeup. This means no blue eyeliner, shimmery lipstick, or body glitter.

- Choose a conservative hairstyle. Pulling your hair back and out of your face gives you a clean and professional look.

- Select a small purse that matches your outfit or bring a briefcase instead.

Casual Date: Business Casual

Casual dates are on the opposite end of the spectrum from a cocktail party. You don't have to wear a suit, but you still need to look your best. During your job search, you should dress business casual only when specified by the company with which you are interviewing.

In the workplace, most organizations define business casual as a collared dress or sport shirt and khaki slacks for men and a blouse or sweater and dress or skirt for women. Shoe styles can vary. Leather loafers and lace-up shoes are most common for men. Flats are most common for women. Unless otherwise noted, always assume that dress for recruiting events and interviews will be business dress.

Accessories Make the Outfit: Interview Must-Haves

Always bring a professional-looking padfolio to your interview. Even though you won't be taking copious notes, it's a good idea to write things down, such as the name of your interviewer, company information, and anything else you find relevant during your interview.

You may even decide to write down questions you want to ask the interviewer beforehand as a safety net in case you get nervous and forget them. A good-quality pad holder usually ranges in price from $30 to $50. All you need is a pad holder large enough to hold an 8½ × 11" tablet and extra copies of your resume.

While you're in the office-supply store, make sure you have a nice, professional-looking pen to take notes with during interviews. You don't have to run out and purchase a solid gold Mont Blanc encrusted with diamonds. Just buy or borrow something nice, a pen that you are certain will write when called on to do so, and one that doesn't have a hotel name on the side...or even worse, the name of a competing company.

Don't go into an interview dressed to the nines and take notes on a napkin with a disposable pen your roommate chewed on, or even worse, have to ask the interviewer for a pen. When I worked in management at a home-improvement center, a man approached me and asked for a job application. After I gave him one, he asked me for a pen. He not only did not get the job, but didn't even get an interview. Forgetting to bring a pen when you're looking for a job is like offering to buy your date dinner and then forgetting to bring your wallet. If you can't remember the bare necessities, that's a strong indicator that you won't make a good employee.

Fashion Tips

- Make sure your shoes are in good shape (no holes) and that they're nicely polished.
- Wear a conservative suit (navy, charcoal, or black).
- Remove unnecessary jewelry and accessories.
- Get an honest opinion of your entire "look" from a friend.

Chapter 7

Getting Ready: Interview Prep

"Well, at least with a crappy job interview I don't have to worry about who's paying for dinner."

—Dave, executive producer, long-running TV sitcom

Think of a first-round interview like a first date. You're typically nervous, and you have no idea what to expect. During a job interview, you're trying to find out more about the potential employer, and the employer is trying to find out more about you. Like dating, where you focus on asking yourself questions such as "I wonder what he's looking for in a girl" or "I wonder if she'll like me," during the interview process you'll also be focusing on whether your skills and abilities are a good fit with the organization.

There is no set number of interviewing rounds a company will hold for a given position, just as there is no limit to the number of dates you will have with a particular person before the relationship is well established. With that being said, two to three rounds of interviews are typical for most companies. When you get past the first round, the interviews get more in-depth as the interviewer tries to further evaluate your knowledge and degree of fit with the company.

It's not enough to just show up for your interview. If you want to have a shot at ultimately receiving an offer, you must research the company and industry, polish your interview skills, and arrive on time (sometimes easier said than done).

Getting to Know You: Gathering Information About the Company and the Job

The Web has made getting to know people a lot easier. From online communities to dating sites, you can learn a lot about people from their personal profiles before you meet them. The Web has also made gathering information about different companies and jobs a lot easier. Most organizations have not only a "jobs" or "careers" section on their Web site, but also an overview of the company and a collection of company-related press releases. Familiarize yourself with this information. Of course, you aren't the only job candidate who will access the Web site when preparing for an interview, so it's critically important that you dig more deeply for information about the company.

> *Fit is very important. People need to know their real strengths and weaknesses when entering a job or a [romantic] relationship. Find the one that best suits you.*
>
> —Bruce, human resources manager

Companies expect you to have done your homework. Plan to look at information from additional sources if you're going to differentiate yourself from other candidates; in the end, that's what you're really trying to do. If you don't stand out in a positive way, your success landing your dream job will be limited. Nobody wants a lifetime of first dates or, in the case of the job search, a lifetime of first-round interviews.

TIP: Sign up for Google Alerts to receive free e-mail updates of relevant Google results based on your topics of interest. Review the news alerts the morning of your big interview so that you have an up-to-date snapshot of the day's business news.

Why Research Is Important

You're trying to accomplish several goals by knowing the facts about your potential employer:

- Impress the interviewer with your intelligence, drive, and knowledge.

- Ensure that you and the interviewer will have plenty of things to talk about.

- Prove to the interviewer that you're really interested in this job—interested enough to do some pretty hardcore research.

The more interest in the company you can demonstrate during the interview, the better. That doesn't mean you should pretend. Faking a high level of interest in a company could ultimately come back to bite you if you receive an offer and end up turning it down. Remember, just as in dating, nobody likes a front or a fake!

Company Financial Information

If you're interviewing with a publicly traded company, take a look at its 10-Q (a quarterly report filed by public companies with the Securities and Exchange Commission that provides a comprehensive overview of the company's state of business) and its annual report, which details business activity for the company over the preceding year. The annual report also contains a letter from the CEO, which might give you an idea of the quality of the organization's management team. To access 10-Q and annual reports, look for a link such as "Investor Relations" under the "Company Information" or "About Us" link on the company's Web site. You can also search 10-Q reports through the Securities and Exchange Commission Web site (www.sec.gov).

Internet Resources

In addition to looking at the company's annual report and 10-Q, you can Google it to locate company-specific articles and important industry information. Also check out Bloomberg.com (www. bloomberg.com) and Yahoo! Finance (http://finance.yahoo.com/) to find other valuable information. Doing so will not only improve your chances during the interview, but will also help paint the most accurate picture of a potential employer, enabling you to make an informed decision if you receive a job offer. A list of online career resources that can assist you in finding such information to prepare for job interviews is included in the appendix.

Enough About You: Let's Talk About Me!

You'll also need to be ready to talk about yourself to convince the interviewer that you're the right candidate for the job. After you have really done your homework on the company, you'll find that it's easier to come up with reasons why you want to work there.

Be ready for the interviewer to ask you why he or she should hire you. With a better understanding of the company and what it's looking for in a job candidate, you can more skillfully tailor your questions and answers to show the interviewer why you're a perfect match.

But just as with a dating situation, you need to carefully navigate the information you've collected. A first date is not the place to reveal, for example, that you know all about the jerk who dumped your date a few years ago. If you appear to know too much about another person, you're likely to make him or her uncomfortable. Similarly, if you're interviewing with a large firm that's currently involved in litigation, the job interview is probably a bad time to say what you think about the legal case.

TIP : A detailed breakdown of interview formats complete with sample questions is included in chapter 8.

Although it is impossible to predict every question you might be asked, start by looking at your resume and preparing to discuss each job you've held. Outline key points you want to make without memorizing possible answers word-for-word. That way, you'll avoid sounding rehearsed. Interviewers are looking for polished candidates who can think on their feet, not candidates who can memorize and recite canned responses to common interview questions on demand. The more you can make the interviewer believe it's the first time you've answered a particular question, even if it's the 100th or 1,000th time, the greater your chances of differentiating yourself from other candidates during your interview.

What happens when you go into a job interview unprepared? Let me tell you a little story. As I mentioned earlier, when I graduated from college, I wasn't sure what I wanted to do. One of my good friends suggested I consider working for an insurance company. My friend offered to arrange an interview, and even though I pretty much knew I wasn't interested, I decided to give it a shot. I put on a suit and grabbed my trusty padfolio. The first question the interviewer asked was "What do you know about insurance?" My heart sank. I started to sweat. I had no idea how to answer that question. I hadn't prepared for the interview.

I thought about bolting for the door, but I didn't want the interviewer to think I was completely insane. I paused for what seemed like an hour but was probably more like 20 seconds. "I know I have some" was my ingenious response. The interview was all but over at that point—yet it dragged on for another 30 painful and awkward minutes.

The moral of the story: Prepare. Even a "practice" interview for a job that you don't think you want will benefit you a lot more if you give yourself an opportunity to do well.

Money and Relationships: How to Handle the Salary Question

How can we talk about dating and relationships and not talk about money? Chances are, when you're on a first or second date and you're asked how much money you make or what kind of car you drive, you're probably going to kick your date to the curb. However, during your job interview, you can't just walk away. At some point, you're going to be asked for "your salary requirement." Some interviewers ask for a specific number, whereas others ask for a range.

Unless the interviewer is making you a formal job offer, it's best to avoid talking about salary. Why? When asking about salary early in the interview process, the interviewer is most likely trying to screen you. Responding with an exact figure can undercut or overshoot the salary for that particular position. On the flip side, when someone asks you how much money you make when you're out on a date, you'll be the one doing the screening.

How should you respond when an interviewer asks about salary without extending a formal offer? By graciously thanking him or her for asking but saying you'd rather wait to discuss salary until after a formal offer is extended. I used this strategy once during a first-round interview, and it worked to perfection.

If you're pressed to give a figure and the interviewer is not going to take no for an answer, respond with an appropriate *range* based on your research using the following resources:

- **The U.S. Department of Labor's Bureau of Labor Statistics** (www.bls.gov) provides detailed wage information by geographic area (national, regional, state, and metropolitan area), occupation, and industry.

- **Salary.com** (www.salary.com) offers a salary wizard that allows you to search for salary ranges by job category and geographic area. You can also purchase a fully customized Personal Salary Report, which provides compensation experts' opinion of your market value based on your experience, education, and performance.

- **JobStar Central** (www.jobstar.org) provides links to more than 300 general and profession-specific salary surveys.

- **The** *Occupational Outlook Handbook,* published by the U.S. Department of Labor, offers information on salary ranges for a number of occupations. After you've gathered information on salary from a number of sources, compare the average range to your offer. Don't forget to factor in cost-of-living differences for different geographic locations.

Me, Myself, and I: Avoiding a Common Interview Pitfall

Have you ever been on a date with someone who talked about him- or herself all night long? Was it like the person was president, treasurer, and secretary of his or her own personal fan club? Let's face it, whether people are on a date or in the workplace, they love to talk about themselves. All too often during the job search, candidates focus too much on what they hope to gain from a potential employer while spending little or no time talking about how the potential employer will benefit from hiring them. "This position will enable **ME** to gain valuable finance experience, while at the same time offering **ME** a great work/life balance and opportunities for **ME** to advance within the organization." Not only is a statement like this incredibly self-centered, it's also too vague and general. A response like this will give the impression that you are thinking only about yourself without any regard for the company. In the world of dating, this would be like telling someone "I want to date you to practice **MY** dating skills so **I'M** better able to position **MYSELF** for future relationships."

Your statement should concentrate on what you're going to contribute to the employer. Tell the interviewer how your skills and abilities will help the company grow its business.

It is important to highlight what you'll bring to the table and why the organization should hire you, but you also want to make sure you balance your answers between what's in it for you and what's in it for the employer. In the preceding example, a better way to respond might be "This position will enable me to gain valuable brand marketing experience while also providing me with an opportunity to use my academic background to make a solid contribution to the firm."

Dating Skills That Work Well During Your Interview

When you're dating, you need to possess certain skills if you're going to have any success. These skills include active listening, communicating, time management, persuasion, negotiation, judgment, and decision making. As luck would have it, these skills also work well during your job interview. Let's look at each skill to see how and why they'll play a role during your interviews (as well as your search as a whole).

- **Active listening:** Giving your full attention to what the other person is saying, nodding, asking questions as appropriate, maintaining eye contact and open body language, smiling, and not interrupting when he or she is speaking are the keys to active listening. Being an active listener makes your interactions with others, both when dating and when looking for jobs, more effective. It increases your chances of making a genuine connection with the person you're speaking with. In a romantic relationship, being an active listener means not staring at the TV when your boyfriend or girlfriend is trying to talk to you. During a job interview, being an active listener means maintaining eye contact, taking limited notes when necessary, and verbally and nonverbally acknowledging what the other person is saying.

- **Communicating:** If you're not able to communicate with others effectively, you're not going to get very far on the dating scene or the job market. Being an effective communicator involves not only what you say, but also how you say it. During a job interview, hand gestures, body movements, facial expressions, and posture can be just as important as the words coming out of your mouth. For example, if a woman asks her boyfriend whether her jeans make her look fat and he says "no" but rolls his eyes, he's in hot water.

- **Time management:** Being able to balance time with your loved ones, work, outside interests, family, and so on isn't something that happens by accident. You have to prioritize tasks and sometimes make difficult sacrifices. The same holds true during your job search when you have to squeeze in time to get ready for an interview or write a bunch of cover letters when you already have a ton on your plate. Identify those things you can postpone and those things you can't.

- **Persuasion:** Persuasion goes hand in hand with negotiation. Say you're in the mood for a movie and your girlfriend or boyfriend wants to play miniature golf. Your ability to persuade your date to change his or her mind will determine whether you'll be eating popcorn or heading for a water hazard. Your ability to persuade an interviewer that you are the right candidate for the job will go a long way in determining whether you get an offer letter or a rejection letter.

- **Negotiation:** Anytime you're dealing with other people, you're going to have differences. Negotiation is part of the give-and-take process of any relationship, whether you're negotiating for more money when you receive a job offer, or you're negotiating with your boyfriend or girlfriend about the possibility of relocating after graduation so that you can go to graduate school.

- **Judgment and decision making:** Two people who can never make up their minds probably won't end up dating for long. After all, they'd probably never be able to figure out what they wanted to do or where they wanted to eat. During your job search and when you ultimately land a job, your judgment and decision making are critical. Which suit should you wear to your big job interview? When offered two jobs, which one is the better fit?

You use the preceding skills every day when you're dating someone. The more you're able to master these skills and exhibit them during your job search, the more success you'll have in finding your dream job.

Polishing Your Dating Skills: Refining Your Interviewing Technique

When you went out on your first date, you were probably nervous, anxious, and worried that you'd mess something up. By the time you went on your fifth, sixth, and seventh dates, you most likely felt more confident in yourself, and your level of pre-date anxiety had probably decreased significantly. Why? Because each date allowed you to practice your dating skills. Yes, even dating requires skills you can refine through repetition and, after each "practice session," self-evaluation to determine areas that need improvement. The same holds true with interviewing for jobs. The only way to refine your skills is through practice.

Caught on Tape: The Benefits of Recording Practice Interviews

Try videotaping a date to see what you're doing right and wrong, and you'll probably end up with a black eye or under arrest—or both. Fortunately for you, when it comes to the job search, recording yourself is far less risky or kinky. Why does a practice interview need to be recorded? Getting a chance to watch yourself interview on film is absolutely the best way to observe your posture (do you slouch? fidget?), hear your own voice (do you mumble?), and gauge your nonverbal signals (do you appear calm and confident?) to look for areas of improvement.

My favorite resource for refining interview skills is www.interview-stream.com. For a nominal fee, InterviewStream gives you the chance to practice, conduct, review, and save your online mock interviews from the convenience of home. All you need is a webcam.

TIP: If you're a college student, check with your campus career center to see whether they offer InterviewStream or the chance to participate in a videotaped mock interview.

Meet Your Mirror Image

You can also prepare for upcoming interviews on your own using a low-tech approach. Try visualizing the interview from your initial handshake to your responses to possible interview questions. Visualize positive interactions and exchanges with the interviewer. Practice your responses to possible questions. Most answers should take about 60 seconds. I've used this technique quite a bit and have found it very helpful. If visualization isn't your cup of tea, try practicing in front of a mirror or go over answers to possible interview questions before you go to bed or while you're in the shower.

Although preparing responses to possible interview questions can be helpful, be sure to keep in mind the discussion about the possible pitfalls of sounding rehearsed during an interview. If you're out of college, contact a close friend or colleague to see whether that person will act as a sounding board for responses you've prepared for possible interview questions.

Give Them a Hand(shake)

As you practice, don't overlook working on your handshake. There are two ends of the spectrum when it comes to a bad handshake—the "vise" and the "dead fish." The vise occurs when your grip is so strong that it actually hurts the other person's hand. The dead fish is when your grip is so limp that your handshake feels like holding a dead fish.

The perfect handshake is firm, falling between the two extremes—not too hard and not too soft. As you're shaking hands, be sure to listen for, and remember, the interviewer's name.

And while we're on the topic of hands, once the interview begins, you'll want to keep them folded on the table in front of you or on top of your opened padfolio in case you want to jot down a few brief notes. If you're a gesturer, try to limit your hand movements somewhat. It's okay to be yourself; you just don't want your gestures to become a distraction.

Make Eye Contact

Equally as important as a firm handshake or where you place your hands during an interview is your ability to maintain positive eye contact with the interviewer. Good eye contact shows that you are confident and poised. Maintaining eye contact doesn't mean getting into a staring contest with the interviewer, but it also doesn't mean keeping your head down or staring out the window.

The Difference Makers: Preparation, Passion, Confidence, and Interpersonal Skills

Recruiters tell me preparation (knowing about both the company and the industry), passion, confidence, and interpersonal skills are all characteristics that differentiate candidates they'll recommend for second-round interviews or extend offers to. Candidates who aren't successful often don't have a basic idea about the company, including what lines of business it's in, how many employees it has, and where its offices are located. Even something as simple as being sure to carefully listen to each and every interview question before you respond can make the difference between getting the job or getting rejected.

I'll See You at 7: How to Arrive at Your Interview on Time, Every Time

Think back to a time when you were getting ready to go on your first date with a new acquaintance. You're on the phone discussing plans for the evening.

"So I'll pick you up at 7?" you inquire.

"Sounds great," your date responds.

"OK, I'll see you then."

There's one problem. You forgot to ask for directions to his or her house. Has this ever happened to you? When it comes to your job search, it's easy to forget to ask for directions or even the location you're expected to go to when scheduling an interview. If a company contacts you to schedule an interview at its office, it is critical that you know how to get there. If you have any questions about directions or other logistics, be sure to ask.

Go on a Trial Run

If you live close to where the interview will be, make a trial run to the spot a few days ahead of time to make sure you can find it. If the interview is too far away and/or you'll be flying in, take advantage of Web sites such as MapQuest (www.mapquest.com) and Google Earth (http://earth.google.com) to plot your course.

Even if you know exactly where you're going and you've been there a hundred times, always leave well enough in advance on the day of your interview to account for traffic jams or other unforeseen delays. Just as you wouldn't want to show up late for a big date, the last thing you want to do is show up late for a job interview and have to explain that you were stuck in traffic or had a flat tire.

Arrive Early

Arrive 15 to 30 minutes before your interview is scheduled to take place. Arriving early shows you're punctual and also allows you extra time to gather your thoughts and fill out any forms (such as an application) the employer asks you to complete. You may even need that 15-minute cushion to find a restroom, stop hyperventilating, grab a cup of coffee, get out of an unexpected traffic jam, or cool down if it's a really hot day.

Speaking of cooling down, I once had to do just that before a job interview. The air-conditioner in my car was broken, it was 100 degrees outside, and I was wearing a suit and tie. By the time I walked to the building from the parking lot, my face was drenched in sweat. Arriving early allowed me extra time to cool down, run to the restroom, and rinse off my face before my interview. You never know when you're going to need that extra 15 to 30 minutes.

Come Prepared

In case an organization does ask you to fill out an application just before the interview, it's a good idea to have an information sheet prepared that includes the names, addresses, and phone numbers of all your former employers, your grammar and high schools, and your college(s) and graduate school(s). Nowadays, you should assume that a potential employer will more or less run a full background check on you, due to security concerns.

In that event, you'll need to be able to supply some truly musty old information about yourself, such as previous addresses and the telephone numbers of personal or professional references. Although your resume contains much of this information, having everything condensed to a one-page document can come in handy. Some applications also ask for the name of your immediate supervisor at each of your previous positions, so have that information on hand as well.

TIP: After you create your reference sheet, you can slip it in the back of your interviewing tablet so that you can easily access it when asked to fill out an application.

Chapter 8

Dinner and a Movie?: Common Interview Formats and Questions

First-round interviews are just like first dates. You worry about what you're going to wear, whether you'll like that person and he or she will like you, and most importantly, whether you'll see your date again if you hit it off.

The options for where you go and what you do on a date are virtually limitless. You can play it safe with dinner and a movie, or you can go dancing at a club or catch a concert or do something completely different. Luckily or unluckily, most job interviews don't offer as many choices. There are four basic interview formats you're likely to encounter, and this chapter describes each of them.

After that, I delve into what to expect on the day of the interview, as well as questions you can ask the interviewer (when she whips out the inevitable "So, do you have any questions for me?"). Then I show you how to close the interview strongly and follow up effectively afterward.

But first, to give you a firm foundation for the interview, I enlighten you about the three basic questions that are at the heart of virtually every job interview.

At the Heart of the Matter

Your ability to effectively address three basic issues during your interview could be just as important in determining whether you get the job as your education, skills, or experience. These three questions are

1. **Why the company?** Why do you want to work for this company above all others? Focus on what makes it different from all the other companies you could work for. Is it the company culture? Is it the reputation? Is it the people? Believe it or not, giant companies have feelings, too. If you say the main reason you want to work there is that it's a top company, that's just like saying you're interested in a prospective date because he or she is hot. Talk about making the company feel special. What about the thousands of other hot people out there? Why not date them? When we're looking for a soul mate, we want someone who "gets us." Someone who understands who we are and what we're all about. Companies want candidates who "get them."

2. **Why the position?** Why are you interested in this particular position instead of other types of positions? Your goal is to show the interviewer

   a. You understand what the job is all about

   b. You are genuinely interested in that position

   c. You can do the job

   Your goal is to convince the employer that you are truly passionate about the opening and qualified to do the job. Make the connection between your skills and experience and the position.

3. **Why you?** Why should the company hire you instead of any other candidate? Focus on your passion for the job; how you will contribute to the company's bottom line; and your skills, abilities, and related experience. Your goal is to convince the employer that you are the best candidate for the job and that hiring you will be worth the money.

The Most Common Interview Types and Formats

Now that we've talked about the importance of being able to address the three whys during the interview process, let's take a detailed look at the most common interview types and formats you're going to face. They include the following:

- **Dinner and a movie—traditional interview:** During this type of interview, you share information about yourself and learn about the other person.

- **Walk down memory lane—behavioral interview:** Behavioral interviews are based on the idea that past behavior can predict future performance.

- **Meet the parents—stress interview:** The stress interview focuses on how you react to stressful situations.

- **Art gallery—case-study interview:** Often more thought-provoking and abstract than some of the previous formats, a case-study interview involves asking you to think through a real business problem.

- **IQ test—interview brain teasers:** Similar to case interviews and often part of them, brain teasers are designed to analyze your thought process as you try to answer abstract questions.

- **Telephone interviews:** Employers often use telephone interviews first as a method of thinning the herd. Then they can call back their favorites for in-person interviews.

- **Group interviews:** Sometimes when you show up for a date, the whole family is sitting there waiting to meet you. Learn how to handle interviews in which you might face a panel of people.

Of course, these types aren't mutually exclusive, so you might have interviews that resemble a mixture of all of them. You might find that you yourself are a stress case before the interview, but if you prepare yourself thoroughly well in advance, you'll do just fine.

The following sections give more details on these main interview types and formats.

Dinner and a Movie: The Traditional Interview Format

When it comes to dates, it doesn't get any more basic and sometimes boring than dinner and a movie. Unless you run out of things to talk about over dinner, there should be few surprises. The same holds true with a traditional interview format. In this type of interview, you are asked basic questions such as "Tell me about yourself." The interviewer will also ask you why you're interested in the position and the company and if you have any questions for him or her.

Sample Traditional Questions

Sample traditional interview questions include the following:

- Walk me through your resume.
- How did you prepare for this interview?
- Where do you see yourself in five years?
- What about this job interests you?
- How would you describe your leadership style?

A traditional interview allows the interviewer to get a feel for the kind of person you are, and in that sense, it's more like a date than other types of interviews. The questions you'll be asked during this type of interview are intended to elicit your honest reactions, to draw you out, and to give you a chance to impress. The point of such an interview is not to grill you on the personal details of your work history, outside interests, or educational background. Many companies conduct traditional interviews because they value teamwork and want to see whether you're the kind of person who'll fit into a team-oriented work environment. And let's be honest: They want to see whether you're likeable because if they hire you, they'll have to see your face every weekday.

When Things Get Personal

Don't get defensive or uncomfortable when a traditional interview leads to a somewhat personal conversation. But at the same time, be careful to steer clear of any discussion that seems too personal to be job-related. Although you should let the interviewer be the one to determine the general subject matter that's discussed during the interview, you have a perfect right to avoid answering questions that are too intimate—just as, on a date, you might change the subject when the other person picks a particularly sensitive conversation topic.

I remember one student I counseled who was asked her marital status during an interview. She responded by saying she didn't believe that question was appropriate and then tried her best to redirect the interview. Despite the awkward exchange, the student decided to finish the interview as quickly and professionally as possible before ultimately pulling herself out of further consideration. Another strategy she could have used would have been to talk about how well the job aligns with her family priorities and, as a result, how she would be able to give full energy to the job and still be available for her family.

If the interviewer continues to ask questions you feel are inappropriate, you can either try to redirect the questions or end the interview immediately, thanking the interviewer for his or her time. Asking personal questions about marital status, religious or political affiliation, race, national origin, age, or sexual orientation is illegal in the United States. Organizations that do so can be sued.

Another potential pitfall to avoid during this type of interview is bad-mouthing other companies. You may have been turned down for interviews by other firms, just as you may have been dumped by more than one boyfriend or girlfriend. The rejection hurt, and it was frustrating. However, the interviewer is not interested in listening to you make negative comments about a past employer. When responding to interview questions, share positive examples, experiences, and comments even if a former employer treated you poorly. If you bring up a negative experience, focus on something that ended with a positive outcome.

Walk Down Memory Lane: The Behavioral Interview Format

When you're on a date and the person you're with starts reminiscing and mentions that the last three serious relationships he or she has been in have all ended terribly, you might start to wonder whether you'll be number four. Why? Because that person's past might be a good predictor of his or her success in a future relationship. This focus on past behavior is at the heart of behavioral interviews. Common questions during this style of interview often begin with "Tell me about a time when...." What the interviewer is looking for is your ability to react to different situations—your behavior when faced with particular challenges.

During a behavioral type of interview, it's important to focus on examples that ended with a positive outcome or those where you learned from your mistake. If you are asked to tell the interviewer about a time when you had to deal with failure, you wouldn't want to provide an example such as "During my first semester of college, I failed calculus and decided to drop out of school," unless you followed up your story by talking about the lessons you were able to take away from that experience and how you would handle the same situation differently today.

What to Expect in a Behavioral Interview

Sample behavioral interview questions include the following:

- Tell me about a time when you had to deal with a difficult situation. How did you deal with it? What were the outcomes?

- Give me an example of a time when you tried to accomplish something and failed.

- Tell me about a time when you were forced to make a difficult decision.

- Describe a situation when you had to persuade others to adopt your idea.

- Tell me about a time when you had too many things on your plate. How did you handle it?

- Give me an example of a time when you took initiative.

The interviewer conducting this type of interview might already believe that your education and experience qualify you for the position. What he or she is looking for is something less tangible than the information on your resume and less personal than the facts you revealed over dinner. The interviewer is trying to develop an idea of how you'd actually perform on the job, so it's very important that you focus on your work or educational experiences. Try to give specific details, such as the specific circumstances leading up to your actions, the year it happened, and so on.

If you were asked to talk about a time when you had too many things on your plate, you'd want to start by describing the situation:

> *Last semester, I was taking a very heavy course load, working a part-time job, and pledging a fraternity.*

Next, you'd discuss how you were able to handle the situation:

> *I prioritized my list of activities to make sure I dedicated enough time to the things that were most important. In this case, grades came first, then work, then the fraternity. By identifying what I needed to do and when, I was able to make the Dean's List, earn some money, and join the fraternity.*

By describing how and why you approached the situation a certain way and what the outcome was, you'll be able to effectively answer behavioral interview questions. If the interviewer asks you to talk about a time when you failed, talk about a time when you met a challenge. For example, maybe you pitched a project at work that didn't receive buy-in. Instead of focusing on the failure, you can talk about how you went back to the drawing board to refine your proposal, ultimately convincing your manager to back the project.

If you don't prepare in advance, a behavioral interview can really lead to a tough, uncomfortable 20 to 30 minutes. One student who asked me for help preparing for a job interview later said that anticipating questions and thinking through possible answers was the best thing she had done to prepare for an interview for a job she eventually landed. Another effective strategy is to take another look at the job description and use it to determine the skills and qualities the interviewer is probably looking for. Once you've identified them, you can work on responses to the "Tell me about…" questions that include these characteristics. For example, if the description mentions "an ability to work under pressure" or "willingness to meet multiple deadlines," it would be appropriate to talk about the time you completed an extremely difficult project for your chemistry class, despite the fact that your lab partner bailed on you at the last minute. It would not, however, be appropriate to admit that you work well under pressure because you never start working on a paper until the day before it's due.

Use the ST.A.R. Method to Answer Questions About Your Experience

The Situation or Task/Action/Result (ST.A.R.) method is another effective strategy for responding to most interview questions that target your previous work experience. When using this method, you must

- Determine what *situation* or *task* you were faced with at a prior job.

- Discuss the *action* you decided to take to resolve the *situation*.

- Conclude your answer by discussing the *result* of your action.

Try to pick examples that ended on a positive note. Employers know there are times when negative outcomes are unavoidable, but during an interview you want to showcase situations in which you made a positive impact. Spend the majority of your time focusing your answer on the action and result instead of the problem. The interviewer is going to be more concerned with how you handled the problem and the outcome than the problem itself.

If you've had more than two jobs, it's also a good idea to pull in examples from each job you've held instead of using the same job over and over. This shows the interviewer you've had meaningful experiences at different jobs you've held. Plus, hearing about different jobs might also help keep his or her attention. Imagine being on a date with someone whose entire conversation revolves around one experience that person had. "When I was living in California…" followed by "Then there was this one time, when I was in California…" followed by "Did I tell you about the time when I was living in California and…." So let me get this straight, you lived in California? Check, please!

Meet the Parents: The Stress Interview Format

Is there anything more nerve-wracking than meeting the parents of the person you're dating for the first time? You're wondering whether they'll like you and you'll like them; whether you'll say all the right things or put your foot in your mouth. You're nervous. Unfortunately, stress interviews can be just as traumatic. During this type of interview, the interviewer will challenge you by firing off questions that are the equivalent of intellectual paintballs. You definitely need to be on your toes during this type of interview because the interviewer's goal is to take you out of your element and to measure your poise under pressure.

No matter what, the key to performing well in this type of situation is to answer calmly, to take everything in stride, and to not be afraid to say that you don't know something. If the interviewer is able to get you worked up, you're playing right into his or her hands. Keep in mind that interviewers who conduct stress interviews are trying to gauge how much you'd be able to contribute to the organization if you had a job involving a great many responsibilities, a lot of deadline pressure, and maybe even an exceptionally demanding boss.

Sample stress interview questions include the following:

- If you could be any animal, what would you be?
- What kinds of people do you like/not like to work with?
- How would you evaluate me as an interviewer?
- Why did you leave your last job?
- How do you handle rejection?
- Tell me about a time when you failed.
- See this pen I'm holding? Sell it to me.
- You don't seem like a very driven person. How are you going to handle this job?
- What would you do if you caught a coworker stealing?

By familiarizing yourself with possible questions, thinking about your responses ahead of time, and remaining poised, you have a chance to show the interviewer first-hand how well you're able to work under pressure.

Art Gallery: The Case-Study Interview Format

Similar to a serious discussion about a fine piece of abstract art with your date, case-study interviews may be quite detailed. In a case-study interview, you're given information about a particular situation or problem and asked to come up with a solution. Consulting firms typically use this interview format, but other industries can also use it. Although coming up with the optimal solution is important, the interviewer probably won't focus on your solution so much as on your ability to think on your feet. To solve the case, follow this method:

- Pay close attention to the information and details you are given.

- Break down the problem into smaller, more manageable parts.

- Prioritize critical issues you want to focus on.

- Analyze the problem using logic, math, and assumptions.

- Make your recommendation.

If you feel you need additional information beyond what was provided, politely ask the interviewer for more details. Don't worry if the interviewer isn't willing to give you more information. He or she knows you're working with limited information and most likely wants to see how well you're able to handle it. Some sample case interview questions include the following:

- You are head of a large corporation. Your company must build a new manufacturing facility. You must decide which country to build the facility in. What factors would you consider?

- A client has engaged us to assist in reorganizing its customer service force. The client wants to cut $30 million in costs from this area over the next three years. What would you cut?

For additional information on case-study interviews, visit Web sites of consulting firms such as Bain and Company (www.bain.com), Boston Consulting Group (www.bcg.com), and McKinsey & Company (www.mckinsey.com) or other companies such as Capital One (www.capitalone.com). InterviewPoint (www.interviewpoint.com) also has sample cases and strategies for answering tough questions. Review the practice cases at its Web site. Familiarize yourself with the way you should structure your response and the types of analysis (costs, revenues, and so on) you might use when formulating your hypothesis.

IQ Test: Interview Brain Teasers

As intellectually stimulating as being on a date with someone with a genius IQ, brain teasers are designed to find out how you approach a problem, not so much to see whether you can guess the right answer to that problem. You'll be tempted to shout out the first answer that comes to mind. Don't. Instead, be aware that the interviewer is trying to determine how you think through a difficult question. Take a few minutes to discuss the brain teaser with the interviewer, in the process revealing your chain of reasoning and your approach to solving it. Are you methodical in your approach to the question? Do you seem to have sound analytical skills as you think through the problem aloud? Are you persistent and self-confident enough to spend some time and energy reasoning it out, or do you throw in the towel and give up? These are the types of qualities the brainteaser might tease out of a job candidate.

Sample brain teaser questions include the following:

- Why are manhole covers round?

- How many dimes would it take to fill up the inside of the Empire State Building?

- How many gas stations are there in the United States?

- Calculate the number of degrees between the hour and minute hands of an analog clock that reads 12:15.

The brain teaser is a good type of sample question to be asked in a mock or practice interview. It can help you develop an appropriate response to a surprise or utterly confounding question. In the event that you are asked a question you can't answer during a real interview (and believe me, it will happen), don't panic. Politely ask the interviewer whether he or she can repeat the question. This gives you extra time to compose your thoughts and come up with an answer. Don't come across as a know-it-all. Sometimes, the best response is to admit that you don't know the answer but that you know several information sources you might consult to find the answer. Although this technique may not always be as effective as giving a well-reasoned answer on the spot, you can also ask the interviewer to come back to that question later in the interview.

By the same token, when you think you have answered a question incorrectly, move on and stay positive. There's no such thing as a perfect interview. Everybody makes mistakes, and the interviewer recognizes that fact. The last thing you want to do is lose your cool and end up jeopardizing your chances just because you couldn't answer one or two questions correctly. The same goes for a date. If something happens to go wrong, say, you arrived at the ticket window too late to get tickets for the movie you'd planned to see together, you and your date are likely to learn a whole lot about each other, just by observing how the other person responds to adverse circumstances.

Companies and dates are both looking for someone they can hire or ultimately settle down with. In a lot of ways, interview questions are not much different from questions you've been asked dozens of times when out on a date. As you prepare for your job interview, think back to those conversations. What worked? What didn't? Did you get a second date?

Long-Distance Romance: Telephone Interviews

Just as you might decide whether you want to go on a date with someone after you've had a chance to talk to him or her over the phone, organizations often use telephone interviews as a way to evaluate candidates before bringing them on site for an interview. Companies conducting telephone interviews do so to save the money they normally would spend covering travel expenses of interviewees and also to narrow the list of potential candidates, thus saving the time normally needed to make travel arrangements and conduct the on-site interviews. Or, sometimes the person calling to arrange an on-site interview may conduct a brief formal or informal telephone interview anyway, to screen out some people and save some time.

When you're contacted by an organization wanting to interview you over the phone, it's always a good idea to schedule something for another day, even if you have time to speak when you receive the call. Rescheduling will enable you to gather your thoughts and the materials you might want to reference during the interview, while also giving you time to find a quiet location where you can take the call without being interrupted. During a phone interview, it's important to behave as if you were face-to-face.

Advantages and Disadvantages of Phone Interviews

There are advantages and disadvantages to telephone interviews. Advantages include the following:

- Interviewing from the comfort of your home without worrying about traveling to the company, getting lost, or being stuck in traffic.

- Not having to put on a suit. Unless your phone has video capabilities, the interviewer won't know whether you're in a suit or wearing shorts. That being said, it's still a good idea to get dressed in something comfortable that instills confidence.

- The ability to access notes, the Internet, and other resources you typically wouldn't be able to reference during an on-site interview.

- The interviewer's inability to read your nonverbal reactions to difficult questions. You also don't have to worry about your handshake or maintaining eye contact.

Disadvantages of telephone interviews include the following:

- Not being able to flash your million-dollar smile or show your enthusiasm for the position the same way you could during a face-to-face interview.

- Not being able to read the interviewer's nonverbal reactions to your answers. During a face-to-face interview, positive nonverbal cues from the interviewer can really improve your confidence and allow you to shine.

- Outside distractions. If you have a noisy roommate or neighbor, you have less control over your environment than you might if you were interviewing in a conference room at the company. Scheduling a time for your telephone interview can help prevent distractions from interfering with your responses. Look for a day and time that you know the dorm or apartment will be quiet or find a different location to take the call.

- The possibility of getting disconnected by accidentally bumping the wrong key or having your battery go dead.

Telephone Interview Tips

Here are a few tips to consider when preparing for a telephone interview. First, if you have call waiting, it's a good idea to disable this feature before the interview starts. You can find instructions on how to do so in the front of most telephone books. Second, while we're talking about phones, it's a good idea to avoid, if at all possible, using your mobile phone for your interview. The chance of dropping a call or hearing static can be much greater with a cell phone than with a traditional land line.

Finally, if you have a desk at your dorm room or apartment, it's a good idea to use it during your telephone interview. If not, a kitchen table can work just as well. Using a desk will allow you to spread out the materials you want to reference during the interview and will also help make the telephone interview feel more formal than it would if you were to be sitting on your bed or couch. You'll also be able to take more notes than you would if you were interviewing on site. You can then pull from those notes to write a personalized thank-you note.

Group Dates: Interviewing with More Than One Person at a Time

Group dates can be something you plan, or they can occur when the person you're getting together with secretly asks a bunch of friends to show up at one of the locations you're planning to visit on your date. Sometimes, what started out as a romantic, one-on-one date can unexpectedly turn into a group outing without warning. The same holds true with job interviews. In many cases, the organization you're interviewing with should provide you with an agenda and a list of people who'll be participating. However, organizations often don't provide this information. Whether you know well ahead of time you'll be interviewing with more than one person, or whether you find this out at the last minute, your approach during the interview should be the same.

To look at group interviews another way, think of them as a series of one-on-one interviews that take place at the same time in the same room. And because you're meeting with more than one person, it's very important that you have extra resumes on hand in the event that one of the interviewers doesn't have a copy. Being able to supply extra resumes will make you look well prepared, as well as confident about the quality of your resume and about your own qualifications for the job. And perhaps even more crucially, if you can hand out extra copies of your materials, you take the important step of including everybody in the interview. A job interview is no time to alienate someone!

TIP: Whether you're dealing with a group on a date or at a job interview, the best thing you can do is relax and be yourself.

Think constantly about ways you can make every participant in the interview feel included. The first step toward doing that is paying close attention to introductions. If you're anything like me, you'll probably forget everyone's name almost as soon as you hear it. Don't allow that to happen! Anytime you can call people by their names, you're that much closer to making friends with them. To avoid forgetting names, jot down the names or initials of each interviewer on your notepad. In addition to making you look thorough and focused, this will help you not only during the interview, but also when you send thank-you notes to follow up.

After the introductions are finished and everyone is seated, it's time for the interview to officially start. As you answer questions, be sure to maintain eye contact with everyone in the room in turn, not just the person asking the question. It's easy to lock in on one person when you're in front of a group, but it's important that you pay attention to everyone. Again, don't let anyone feel left out. Be pleasant and smile at everyone. If you get the opportunity to strike up a brief conversation with an individual, by all means, do so—as long as it doesn't exclude everyone else. For example, if someone tells you he attended your alma mater, express interest, but don't immediately launch into a round of "did you know So-and-So?"

If you have a half-day of interviews scheduled at the same company, you'll usually have a chance to take a break at some point during the day. Even if you're not thirsty or you don't need a restroom break, take full advantage of any break time to gather your thoughts and jot down notes. If you don't take a break, it's hard to maintain your concentration and energy throughout the day. Whether you're dealing with a group on a date or at a job interview, the best thing you can do is to relax and be yourself.

So, Tell Me About Yourself: Questions You Can Ask During Your Interview

Good two-way conversation is a key to any date. Remember the discussion about the common dating pitfall of me, myself, and I from chapter 7? One person shouldn't do all the talking. Interviews are much the same. Before and even during the course of your interview, you'll want to come up with questions you'd like to ask the interviewer(s). In almost every case, you'll be asked whether you have any questions near the end of your interview. This is not just the interviewer's attempt to be polite. Your ability to ask well-thought-out questions can say a lot about you and can have a direct impact on your eventual success in making it through the interview process, including whether or not you'll ultimately receive a job offer. If a good question occurs to you during the interview and you have an opportunity to write it down without disturbing the flow of the conversation, by all means, do so.

> "In dating, I've learned that when a person is nervous, he tends to talk too much about himself and not focus on his date as much as he would if he were not engaged in nervous chatter. To keep myself from doing this, I plan out certain questions in my mind that I can ask to show interest in my date. In job interviews, asking the interviewer questions shows the same type of interest and makes a similarly good impression."
>
> —Marcy, legal assistant

Although there's no set number of questions to ask your interviewer, you should have three to five good ones prepared ahead of time. When you select a question from your list, pay close attention to what has been covered during the interview so that you can avoid asking about something that has already been addressed. It's important to appear to have absorbed the information the interviewer has provided.

What Makes a Good Question?

To develop effective questions, you'll need a firm understanding of the company, the industry it's in, and the position you are interviewing for. Anyone can ask "What's a typical day like?" without doing any research on the company or the position at all. The more you are able to ask intelligent questions that show you've done your homework, the more successful you'll be. Your questions will vary for each interview, but, in general, you should focus on questions that show the interviewer you're goal-oriented and that you understand the needs of the company or organization. But also consider questions that provide answers you really want to hear about.

Never ask about salary during the early rounds of the interview process. Focus on questions about job content and the organization, including any recent positive news that might have made the headlines. If the interviewer is seriously interested in you as a candidate, he or she will initiate the discussion about salary when the time is right.

TIP: Develop questions that assume a best-case scenario—that you're offered the job. For example, if the job would require you to relocate to another city, ask a question that shows you've already started doing research on the new city (and have liked what you've read) but want to know more.

As mentioned earlier, I recommend writing down your questions on the tablet in your notepad holder. You definitely should have them memorized, but having them written down can provide a security blanket if you get nervous and forget what you wanted to ask.

Sample Questions to Ask

Sample questions you can ask the interviewer(s) include the following:

1. What are the immediate challenges the candidate selected for this position will face?

2. Can you describe the traits you look for in a colleague?

3. How would you describe your management style (if the interviewer would be your manager)?

4. Does your company or organization encourage on-the-job creativity?

5. How is employee performance evaluated?

6. How would you describe your organizational culture?

7. Are there opportunities to further my education/training?

8. Does your company promote from within?

9. Do you encourage participation in community or professional activities, such as volunteer organizations or professional associations?

10. Why do you enjoy working for the company?

Asking questions also gives you the chance to reiterate key points that you made, or neglected to make, during the interview. Say, for example, you ask sample question 2 from the preceding list. After the interviewer has answered the question, you can follow up with examples that show you possess those traits. In the extremely rare case in which all your questions have been answered during the interview, ask the interviewer to clarify a point made earlier or to be more specific about a topic such as organizational culture.

Asking for Feedback

Often candidates feel the urge to ask for feedback at the end of a date or a job interview. Although it might seem like a good idea at the time, asking for feedback will probably only hurt your chances for a second date or a second interview. Nobody wants to be put on the spot…especially if things didn't go well. Moreover, in some cases interviewers might be bound by company policy not to provide interview feedback.

To look at this situation differently, think about how you'd feel if you were on a first date with someone and as the night was drawing to a close, the person asked you for specific feedback on the date beyond "So, did you have a good time?" If you had a miserable time, would you want to respond to your date when asked for feedback? Of course, all's not lost. There are ways you can try to solicit interview feedback, and the "When the One You Love Is in Love with Someone Else:

Bouncing Back When You Don't Get an Offer" section in chapter 9 addresses them.

The more you prepare for your interview, the better your chances for success. Try to find out which industries/companies use each interview format (for example, consulting and investment banking often use case interviews). By doing so, you'll know what to expect and how to respond, and that will let the interviewer know you've really done your homework.

The Big Date: Your Job Interview

Now that you've read about different interview formats and interview preparation strategies, it's time to walk through a possible interview scenario. Let's say you've been contacted by one of the companies you applied to and the employer wants you to interview at its office in Houston, Texas. You've done your research on the company, you've spent time anticipating possible interview questions, and you're prepared for all the different interview formats. You arrive at the company's office at 8:40 a.m., and you're now waiting in the reception area for your interview.

> *Anticipation [before a job interview] is pretty similar to a first date, but you have to know that the more times you interview/date, the easier it will get.*
>
> —Jake, research analyst

All Eyes on You

From here on out, all eyes are on you. And I mean that literally. If the organization has a receptionist on duty, he or she very well could be evaluating you from the moment you walk in the door. Did you introduce yourself? Were you friendly? The 15 to 20 minutes you spend with this person could leave a lasting impression. It may bring back memories of those awkward moments waiting for your date to get ready while chatting with his or her parents in their living room, but don't let potential awkwardness unnerve you or put you off your game. Those parents were interviewing you to ensure that you were fit company for their son or daughter! The same holds true for each person you meet when you go on site for an interview.

At 9:07 a.m., the interviewer walks into the lobby and introduces herself. "Hi, I'm Jane Smith" she says. "Hi, Jane [you can also use Ms. Smith, depending on how she introduces herself]. I'm Carl Doe," you reply as you shake hands. After some small talk in the lobby, Jane escorts you to the room where you'll be interviewing. Be sure to wait until she offers you a seat before sitting down and be sure to maintain an upright posture once you are seated. I've seen some pretty funky chairs over the years, and I know it can sometimes be difficult to sit comfortably while still maintaining good posture, but do your best. If there's room, open your notepad holder and take out a pen so that you can take notes. You should minimize your note taking overall so that you don't distract yourself or the interviewer. Try to limit your note taking to key information you feel will come in handy later as you are asking the interviewer questions, writing thank-you notes to follow up after the interview, and evaluating different job offers.

Don't Fake It

During the interview, you definitely want to show passion and enthusiasm for the position. But, at the same time, you don't want to come across as something you're not. If you're not a cheerleader (all smiles and spirit fingers) or don't have a great sense of humor (*a la* Dave Chappelle), that's okay. That's who you are. It's better to be yourself during the interview (while always being professional, of course) and let the chips fall where they may than it is to modify your behavior and then find you're not a good fit with the company two months into the job.

Play to Your Strengths

Just as you wouldn't call attention to the pimple that showed up smack-dab in the middle of your forehead during a first date, you don't want to bring up your weaknesses during your interview. If the interviewer asks you about weaknesses, it's okay to mention them and talk about what you're doing to address them. But don't go into the interview apologizing for a lack of experience or for not having a certain skill. Focus on the experience and skills you do have. For a list of common interview questions and their dating equivalent, check out table 8.1.

Table 8.1: Common Interview Questions and Their Dating Equivalents

Interview Question	Date Question
Walk me through your resume.	Tell me about yourself (also a common interview question).
Where do you see yourself in five years?	Are you looking for a long-term relationship?
Where else are you interviewing?	Are you dating anyone?
Are you willing to relocate?	Are you from around here?
What do you look for in a job?	What types of people do you normally date?
Have you had any related internships or previous work experience?	Have you ever been in a serious relationship?

At the end of the interview, Jane should give you a chance to ask the questions you prepared ahead of time and be willing to discuss the next steps in the interview process. If she doesn't discuss next steps, it's okay to ask. The important thing here is not to paint her into a corner by asking whether you will receive a second-round interview, but rather for you to get an idea of the time frame and the process (that is, will there be second-round interviews, and when will they take place?).

Going for the Goodnight Kiss: How to Close the Interview Strong

The close of an interview is a lot like the end of a date. You're nervous, often wondering whether the person you're with wants to give you a romantic goodnight kiss, the "let's be friends" hug, or the always-disappointing "don't call me; I won't call you" handshake. Although you'll never, and I repeat *never*, actually go for a goodnight kiss at the end of an interview, there are some things you can do to seal the deal.

- **Reaffirm your interest in the position** (the equivalent of "call me"). Doing so lets the interviewer know that you're still very much interested in the job. Start by highlighting two to three reasons why you're the right candidate. Also be sure to repeat why you're interested in working for that particular company; what makes it uniquely different? Saying you want to work for the company because it's an industry leader isn't enough; there could be a different industry leader tomorrow. Although your answer will vary for each company, people and corporate culture might be at the top of the list.

- **Ask about next steps in the interview process** (the equivalent of "will I see you again?"). Knowing when the company plans to notify candidates of whether they made it to the next round of interviews can be incredibly valuable. Knowing the time frame not only helps ease some of your anxiety so that you're not waiting by the phone for weeks on end, but also is something you can refer to if you decide to follow up if you haven't heard from the company.

In addition to closing strong, you'll also want to spend some time shortly after your interview to reflect on how you thought everything went. Even though analyzing your interview performance can be just as stressful as a sleepless night wondering whether the person you went on a date with earlier that night likes you as much as you like him or her, it's something you must do if you want to improve your interview skills. Don't agonize over every sentence you uttered during the interview. Instead, assess the interview calmly and rationally. Reflecting on your interview while it's fresh in your mind helps you identify the things you think you did well and the things you might need to work on before your next interview. And it will also help you write your personalized thank-you note to show the interviewer you appreciated his or her time.

Waiting by the Phone: Sending a Thank-You Following Your Interview

Unlike the world of dating, where you might wait a few days before calling the person you just went out with, when it comes to your job search, prompt follow-up is everything. To maximize your chances of landing the job, you can't afford to wait to follow up. Send your thank-you note within 24 to 48 hours after the interview.

Why should you send a thank-you note after a job interview? Say you're competing against another applicant and have almost identical backgrounds. Following the interview, your competitor sends a thank-you note or e-mail message and you don't. It sounds arbitrary, but the follow-up note could be one of the things the interviewer uses to differentiate you from the other candidate. I know I said some recruiters don't care about thank-you notes in chapter 4, but I also said some do.

Because your thank-you note shows that you have good manners and also reminds interviewers that you're still interested in the job, the time frame for sending it is very important. Make sure your thank-you note is in their hands before they make their final decision. In some cases, interviewers are worried that the candidate they really want to hire will turn them down.

> *It is very important to contact someone after a date or an interview. If you're not interested, that's fine…still validate the person. All great successes come from taking the bad and creating something good. A tip that helped me get where I am now: Never burn bridges and never lose touch with prospective employers, even if they didn't give you an offer. As for dating, calling (even if you're not interested) keeps the friendship open…which is a much better alternative.*
>
> —Jennifer, assistant account executive

Don't forget that one of the organization's main goals going into the interview was to gauge how enthusiastic you are about the position and how likely you are to accept it. The thank-you note, in this case, functions just like the phone call you make within a day or so of a date that went well. No follow-up in such a case clearly means you're not interested in pursuing a relationship. Recognize that the same rule may apply to a job interview.

Your thank-you can be a handwritten note, a typed letter, or an e-mail. Deciding on which format to use depends on how nice your handwriting is, how fast you want to get the thank-you in the interviewer's hands, and whether there is a preferred format for that industry (for example, someone in technology might prefer e-mail to a typed letter). When sending a handwritten note, most people prefer to use monogrammed stationery or purchase thank-you cards that are blank inside. If you're going to type your thank-you, consider printing it on quality resume paper and sending it in a matching No. 10 envelope. See figure 8.1 for a sample of a thank-you letter sent after an interview.

22 Moorefield Avenue
Gainesville, FL 32611
(Date)

Ms. Anne Jenkins
Director
Acme Services Unlimited
8520 Glimsher Boulevard
Gainesville, FL 32611

Dear Ms. Jenkins:

Thank you for meeting with me on Monday, May 20, 200x, to discuss the management opening currently available at Acme Services Unlimited.

As I mentioned during the interview, I am very excited about the opportunity and I believe my prior management experience and extensive background in manufacturing fit perfectly with the position currently available. I particularly enjoyed our discussion about the impact of future government regulations and how they can potentially lead to new opportunities for growth for Acme Services.

Again, thank you for your time and consideration. I look forward to hearing from you.

Sincerely,

Bill Stevens

Bill Stevens

Figure 8.1: Sample thank-you letter.

As mentioned earlier, the thank-you letter you write should be relatively short (two or three brief paragraphs of two to three sentences each). You want to thank the interviewer for taking time to interview you, reiterate your interest in the position, cover any important points you want to make (about your qualifications, or even about your continuing interest in the job), and close on a positive note. Although it takes some work, I recommend individualizing each thank-you note you send, whether you interviewed with one person or a large group. This gives your note a personal touch that most people neglect.

If you weren't able to get a business card from the interviewer, you can always try locating a general number on the company Web site and then calling to ask for the interviewer's contact information. You can tell the operator or receptionist that you have some materials you would like to send to that person and that you want to make sure you have the correct spelling of his or her name and the correct mailing address.

TIP: If you were able to take notes about key topics that the interviewer or interviewers discussed, incorporate that information into your letter. If you and the interviewer discussed a relatively personal matter, such as the fact that you're a big fan of the local sports franchise, you might mention that as well.

In your closing paragraph, you'll want to thank the interviewer again for his or her time and consideration and indicate that you look forward to hearing from him or her in the future. If you're typing your letter and printing it, don't forget to sign your name (preferably in black ink because it looks more professional). If you're sending a thank-you via e-mail and you have an automatic signature that lists your complete mailing address including your name, it's still important to include a complimentary closing such as "Regards" followed by your name to give your e-mail that personal touch.

Chapter 9

Getting Serious: Accepting, Negotiating, and Declining Job Offers

"Ultimately jobs are like marriages; it has to work for both parties or someone is going to cheat, get fed up, and leave. There are plenty of different companies to work for; find one that shares your sense of work ethic, etc."

—Kate, president, human resources consulting firm

After you've gone on a number of dates with someone, your relationship with that person starts getting serious. You stop dating other people. The same holds true with your job search. After you've had one or more rounds of interviews with different companies, they'll start making job or internship offers to the candidates they like. This time can be both exciting and stressful as you wait to hear from organizations that interest you.

This chapter goes into detail about how to decide which offer to accept, how to negotiate pay and benefits, how to let a company down gently, and how to pick up the pieces when you get rejected.

Only Fools Rush In: Responding to Job Offers

When a company does call to extend you an offer, don't feel as though you have to accept or reject it on the spot. In most cases, the representative who contacts you will expect you to want some time—usually a few days—to think about the offer. If you're interested in the position, let the company know you're excited about the opportunity and ask if it would be possible to have some additional time to think about the offer. Every company is different, but most should be willing to give you one to two weeks to get back to them. If you're not interested in the opportunity, you don't want to burn any bridges. It's still a good idea to ask for a day or two to think about the offer so that the organization knows you were thoughtful enough to consider your options instead of just rejecting it on the spot.

Asking for more time not only allows you to think about the offer on the table, but can also give you a chance to hear back from others you've interviewed with. However, once you ask for more time, you pretty much have to make up your mind within that time period, even if you haven't heard back from other companies to which you've applied. Asking for another extension could be viewed negatively; you agreed to make your decision and get back to the company by the specified time, and now you appear to be indecisive or even devious. If you have an offer deadline but you're still hoping to hear from another firm, you're most likely going to have to choose between the offer you have in hand (the sure thing) or the chance at an offer from the other company (the leap of faith). Your ultimate decision will depend in large part on how much risk you are willing to take.

Depending on your individual situation, you might feel compelled to accept the first offer that comes along, just as you might latch onto the first person who shows a romantic interest in you out of the fear of being alone. On the other hand, you might decide to wait until you find the job you really want, just as you might "play the field" until you find the person you know you want to be in a serious relationship with.

TIP: Although accepting the first job or person that comes along might seem like a good idea at the time, in the long run, it's often best to find the job or person that is "Mr./Ms. Right," not "Mr./Ms. Right Now."

In some cases, you might have to decide on one offer before you've had a chance to hear from other organizations you've interviewed with. Whether you decide to accept that offer is entirely up to you. Doing so takes you out of the running for other offers that might come along a day, a week, or a month after you've accepted another position. Because of this risk, it's very important for you to think through how your decision will affect you now and also how it will affect your career path in a few years. For example, say you receive an offer from your second-choice firm while you're waiting to hear back from your first-choice firm. Depending on how much time your second choice is willing to give you to decide, you might have to accept or decline this offer before you've had a chance to hear from your first choice.

Some clients ask me if it's okay to change their mind after they've already officially accepted an offer. In almost every case, the answer is no. If you accept your second choice and your first choice makes you an offer a few days later, the last thing you want to do is go back on your acceptance. Along those same lines, it's never okay to accept more than one full-time job offer at the same time. As long as polygamy is illegal, so, too, should be accepting multiple offers.

Unfortunately, uncertainty is often a part of the job search process. Because we can't predict the future, we often have to make decisions based on the information we have at the time. Reneging on an offer you've already accepted is like cheating on someone you're dating. When you cheat on someone, you're a creep. When you renege, you look very bad.

How Do You Know If a Job Is Mr. or Ms. Right?

Sometimes you just know. It was love at first sight. You have a good feeling about the people you'll be working with, the money and location are right, and the job content is exactly what you're looking for. However, sometimes the decision isn't as easy. So how do you know if a job is Mr. or Ms. Right? If your answers to all the following questions are "yes," then maybe it's time to sign on the dotted line.

- Does the company or organization offer the opportunity and job content I'm looking for?

- Am I really a good fit for the job and with the organization's culture?

- Did I get along with the people I met during the interview process?

- Are the salary and compensation package what I was looking for?

- Can I see myself working there? With those people? In that building?

- Will the job provide opportunities for career advancement?

- Does the job offer a healthy work/life balance?

- Am I planning to take this job for the right reasons, or am I settling for something that won't make me happy—not even temporarily?

Notice that I said "if you answered 'yes' to *all*," not just a few, of the questions. When you find the right job, it's usually going to be a total package. It's not just the money or the location or the job content, but all those things and more.

If you receive two offers for positions that are almost identical (title, content, chances for career advancement, and so on), the choice might not be as difficult as it would be if your second choice wasn't closely related to your future career plans. Let's say you wanted to work in marketing, but the offer you received was in finance. Start by looking at the long term. Will accepting a position in finance enable you to pursue your real career interest down the road, or will you be pigeonholed into a career track based on the job function you are currently in? Will you make valuable contacts via your finance job, and will you gain valuable experience that might help you start a marketing career when the time is right? Unfortunately, there's no way to know for sure, but you can talk to people who work in marketing to get a sense for what backgrounds and career experiences are most valued in their field. And you also should consider the possibility that you'll love the job in finance and never think about marketing again!

For a handy resource designed to help you evaluate your offer(s), refer to the *Job Offer Evaluation Worksheet* in the appendix.

How Do You Know If a Job Is Mr. or Ms. Wrong?

Just as you know when a job offer just seems to feel right, likewise sometimes you know when one doesn't. Maybe you didn't get a good feeling about the people you'll be working with, the money and location weren't where you wanted them to be, or the job content wasn't what you were looking for. If deciding on the job offer isn't cut and dry, revisit the preceding questions. If you answer "no" to most or all of the questions, it might be time to turn down that job offer.

After you've carefully weighed your options, you'll need to decide which job offers seriously interest you. Although there is no universal method for deciding on different job opportunities, most people I've spoken with over the years will tell you to "trust your gut," and I would have to agree with them. More than likely, you'll know which situation is the right fit for you based on the information you gathered during your job search and by your answers to the preceding questions. However, nothing in life is 100 percent certain. Sometimes your gut instinct will be right, and other times it might be wrong. Of course, in addition to the always-helpful self-knowledge you've gained during the job search, the possibility of negotiating the offer can also be an important factor in your decision-making process, and I talk more about that in the next section.

What About *My* Needs In This Relationship?: Negotiating Your Job Offer

When you're in a romantic relationship, sometimes you have to negotiate with your significant other when you feel your needs aren't being met. Maybe you want to spend a weekend in Vegas with your friends, but your boyfriend or girlfriend wants you to spend the weekend with him or her. You mention the reasons you feel the trip is important, and your boyfriend or girlfriend counters with why he or she feels it is important for you to stay home. When it comes to negotiating a job offer, the process is similar. You have an idea of what you'd like to make, the company has an idea of what it would like to pay you, and you both provide justifications for how you came to your conclusions.

Unfortunately, if you are someone who is about to or has just graduated from college, the opportunity to negotiate your starting salary is fairly limited. Some employers vary offers based on years of relevant full-time work experience, the prestige of your undergraduate institution, your GPA, and so on. With this in mind, when you receive a job offer, you'll need to decide whether you want to negotiate your compensation package. If attempting to alter the initial terms of the offer is something you decide to do, it's important that you try to determine whether the company is willing to negotiate before moving any further. Some companies won't negotiate at all, whereas others are more flexible. Organizations that don't negotiate are usually in very competitive sectors or government, where they must spend a great deal of time benchmarking offers against those of their competitors.

Sample Script: Calling to Negotiate a Job Offer

You: "Good afternoon [insert his or her first name]. This is [insert your name].

"I am very excited about the opportunity to work as an investment banking analyst with BRC Securities. Since our last conversation, I have had a chance to look over my formal offer letter, and I have a question regarding the compensation package.

"According to employment data from the National Association of Colleges and Employers for last year's graduating class, the average starting salary for investment banking analysts in the Northeast was $55,000. I know the base salary outlined in the offer letter was $43,000."

Company Representative:

"Unfortunately, we don't have much flexibility. Our budget won't allow us to deviate much from the base salary you were offered."

Your Possible Response:

"I appreciate the challenges of having to work within budgetary constraints. However, I believe my summer internship experience with UBS Investment Bank and my strong financial modeling skills differentiate me from other candidates. I am positive this experience will enable me to make an immediate positive contribution to your bottom line."

OR

"I appreciate the challenges of having to work within budgetary constraints. I asked because I have a competing offer in an area with a lower cost of living."

Company Representative:

"Let me talk to my colleagues. Can I get back to you by the end of the week?"

You: "Thank you very much. I am very excited about the offer and look forward to hearing from you later this week."

How Open to Negotiation Are They?

How can you find out whether a company will negotiate? It's not an exact science; most people prefer not to talk about salaries or any other type of compensation, so it can be hard to gather data on a company's willingness to give in certain areas. If you are a college student, you can check with your campus career office to see if the staff know whether certain companies have been willing to negotiate in the past. They should also have average salary information for specific industries. In addition to your campus career center, family members and close friends who work for the company could also be helpful.

Know the Range

Before you approach the organization to discuss its offer, it's essential to have a firm grasp of the pay range and benefits typically offered by the industry and company you're considering. Although salary information is easier to come by than information about vacation time or whether a company will cover your relocation expenses, you should definitely not rule out negotiating for things other than salary. You may want a particular perk, such as the use of a laptop or a paid cellular phone plan, or even the use of a company car. If these demands aren't too outlandish for this particular industry or sector, it may not hurt to ask about them—especially if having these things will enhance your job performance. A sample script for calling to negotiate your job offer is included earlier in this section.

NOTE: Salary is one of the many items you might want to try to negotiate. Others include bonuses, benefits, paid vacation time, reimbursement for related expenses, and perks (parking, company car, and so on).

As mentioned in chapter 7, there are a number of great resources to assist you in locating salary data. The U.S. Department of Labor's Bureau of Labor Statistics (www.bls.gov) provides wage information by geographic area (national, regional, state, and metropolitan area), occupation, and industry. Salary.com offers a salary wizard that allows you to search for salary ranges by job category and geographic area. In addition, JobStar Central (www.jobstar.org) has links to more than 300 general and profession-specific salary surveys. The *Occupational Outlook Handbook*, published by the U.S. Department of Labor, also offers information on salary ranges for a number of occupations.

Although base salary is an important part of any job offer, don't overlook the value of other forms of compensation. In the United States, wages and salaries typically represent 70 percent of employer spending on compensation, with benefits making up the remaining 30 percent. This means that if your base salary is $40,000 per year, your employer-paid benefits will likely come in at around $12,000, which is not chump change, by any means.

Being in Love Does Have Its Benefits: Employee Benefits and Other Forms of Compensation

When you're in love, the intellectual and emotional benefits you receive from being in that relationship go far beyond basic physical attraction. You have someone with whom you can share yourself. On the job market, benefits can also be very important. They can account for a significant part of your total compensation package. Let's look at possible benefits and other compensation that employers offer and discuss why they might be something to consider when evaluating different job offers:

- **401(k)s:** As part of your retirement package, organizations often offer you the option of investing in a 401(k), a retirement account that allows you to make tax-exempt contributions straight out of your paycheck, up to a maximum yearly amount. Many of these organizations also match 25 to 100 percent of the money you put in up to a company-set limit. Matching contributions may be subject to vesting, meaning that you might need to work for the company for a specified number of years before matching contributions are yours to keep. If the organization you're negotiating with doesn't match contributions, you might decide you want to negotiate to see whether it will.

- **Stock options:** If you're going to work for a publicly traded company (a company that sells its stock in the public markets), stock options can also be an attractive part of your benefits package. Stock options offer employees the opportunity to purchase shares of stock at a discounted rate, lower than the market rate. They're called *options* because you don't have to purchase the stock; you can instead keep the options for a lengthy period of time until you think you can sell the stock for the price you want.

- **Stock-purchase plans:** Similar to stock options, but with different rules, stock-purchase plans often give you a chance to enter a pool with other employees to actually purchase company stock at a lower price. You can then immediately sell the stock for a small, predictable gain. There's not much to negotiate if the company does offer such a plan, unless it plans to exclude you from joining for a few months to make sure you're planning to stick with the company.

- **Health insurance:** If you're a college student, you're probably covered under your parents' health insurance until you reach a certain age. After that, it's up to you to find coverage. If you have a family, or if you're single and in need of ongoing medical care, not having or having limited medical coverage could cost you thousands of dollars per year. The out-of-pocket costs of hospital stays, prescription drugs, and doctor appointments can be staggering. Take a look at what coverage the company offers. Does it offer health coverage? If it does and you need coverage for your family, find out if including family members in the coverage is going to cost you a lot of money. Typically, organizations offer full-time employees health plans that consist of a combination of employer and employee contributions.

- **Life and disability insurance:** Many organizations also offer life and disability insurance; although these insurance packages may provide only modest amounts in the event of a catastrophe, don't overlook these benefits. Depending on your age and marital status, such insurance may be extremely important to protect you and your family. When considering job offers, ask yourself whether you want to shell out the monthly fees for this type of coverage or whether you'd prefer that your employer pick up the tab.

- **Signing bonus:** Companies in certain highly competitive industries (typically consulting or investment banking) may offer a one-time signing bonus to entice you to join their organization. This bonus is in addition to your base salary. Signing bonuses can sometimes be as much as a few thousand dollars.

- **Year-end bonus:** Different from a signing bonus, a year-end bonus is tied to the company's profitability, your productivity, or both. The year-end bonus can be either a percentage of total revenues or profits or a flat dollar amount.

- **Relocation expenses:** If you accept a position that requires you to move to another city, state, or country, reimbursement for relocation expenses could save you thousands of dollars. Not all companies offer to reimburse you for your expenses as part of their standard compensation package. When they don't, ask whether that is something they would be willing to consider. When they do offer to cover your expenses, don't be afraid to negotiate the dollar amount if you feel their figure isn't equitable. And by equitable, I don't mean whether the company is willing to cover the cost of flying your cat from Georgia to California. (Believe it or not, I once counseled a client who considered asking just that. As I told her, the last thing you want to do is jeopardize a great job opportunity over a few hundred dollars...especially when that few hundred dollars is for a plane ticket for a cat.)

But I Thought You Loved Me! When Your Job Offer Isn't What You Expected

Have you ever been in a relationship in which it seemed as though you cared more about the person you were with than he or she cared about you? Whether you were right or wrong, when you have certain expectations and those expectations aren't met, you feel hurt. It's no different during your job search. If you were hoping for a certain salary and your offer is lower than what you expected, you're going to feel hurt.

If your offer isn't in line with the average salary range for someone with your experience and skill set, approach the person who made you the offer to see whether there is any room for negotiation. How should you approach this sensitive topic? Don't ask for more money because you have student loan payments, an expensive relocation to undertake, or a baby on the way. Organizations want to know what you're going to bring to the table that's worth the extra money. They don't care about personal expenses you're going to incur. Think about why you're *worth more* than what's been offered before you contact the company.

In some cases, having another offer also increases your bargaining power. However, when mentioning a competing offer, be careful not to sound threatening; doing so might turn off the employer you're negotiating with. Before you know it, what was a promising offer could end up being pulled off the table.

If the person is willing to negotiate, stress what you will add to the company's bottom line while citing accurate salary figures that someone with your educational background and experience should expect to make within that industry. Look for common ground. Even if the company representative is totally willing to negotiate, if he or she has offered you $40,000 and you think you're worth $70,000, chances are you're both going to have to try to meet in the middle.

NOTE: The person you're talking to may not be able to make a decision on the spot and may legitimately have to get back to you after checking with someone else at the company.

Start your conversation by expressing your pleasure at receiving the offer. After you have done this, mention that there is one area you'd like to discuss before going forward. To avoid creating ill will, don't use potentially inflammatory or insulting phrases like "I'm worth way more than that" or "If you can't pay me *X* amount, I'm afraid I'm going to have to look at other options."

Don't pursue a salary or benefits negotiation unless the elements lacking in the initial offer are truly the major factor keeping you from accepting the position. The last thing you want to do is ask for a certain salary or benefits package and have the company work hard to make it happen, only for you to turn around and say you don't want the job after all.

When you've arrived at mutually agreed-upon terms, it's time to verbally accept the offer. Be sure to indicate the specifics of the position you're accepting, including the title, starting salary, and start date. After you've accepted verbally, the company should provide you with an offer letter that outlines the terms and conditions of employment, including your starting salary and benefits. Until you receive the offer in writing, nothing has been finalized. When you get the offer letter, make sure you look it over carefully before you sign it. And before you put the signed offer letter in the mail, be sure to make a copy for your files.

If We Don't Get Engaged Before Christmas, We're Through! Exploding Job Offers

In a sense, an exploding offer is similar to your long-term boyfriend or girlfriend giving you an ultimatum. In most cases, coercion isn't the way to start off right, whether it's on the job or in a relationship. Although shotgun weddings are not as common as they once were, every once in a while a company will extend an exploding offer to a candidate. It's referred to as an "exploding offer" because all or part of the offer will disappear if the offer is not accepted by a certain deadline.

Exploding offers are typically not good for the employer or the potential employee. As a candidate, you want enough time to gather information so that you are able to make an informed decision as to whether the position is right for you. Likewise, it's in the employer's best interest to make sure the people it hires are going to add value to the organization.

It's Not You, It's Me: Turning Down a Job Offer

Unless you plan on accepting every offer you receive, at some point you're going to have to dump somebody. This is typically one of the most difficult things you'll have to do during your job search…especially when you've spent a lot of time getting to know people at the company during the interview process. Why can turning down an offer be so difficult? Nobody wants to be the bearer of bad news. Calling an organization to say you've accepted a position with another company is a lot like telling someone you can't go out with him or her because you already have a date or are in a committed relationship with someone else. In both cases, the other party will feel rejected, disappointed, or even angry (see figure 9.1).

THE BREAKUP

It's not you, it's me.   Is there someone else?
I can change!

Figure 9.1: The breakup.

When you're turning down an offer, it's best to call the person who extended you the offer directly to let him or her know. To avoid burning bridges, you will want to keep your conversation short but not abrupt. Thank the person for the opportunity. Let him or her know (in general terms) why you've decided to turn down the position. For example, are you rejecting it for a position that is more in line with your long-term career interests? Are you doing it to be closer to family? You want to be general to avoid making any negative comments about the company; these comments might come back to hurt you later if you want to apply for a position in the future. In the world of dating, you probably wouldn't like it much if somebody pointed out all the reasons he or she didn't want to go out with you. The same holds true when you're turning down a job offer.

You also don't need to mention the name of the other company you're going to work for, just as you wouldn't want to tell the person you're rejecting the name of your new love interest. "I wanted to let you know I have accepted a position with another organization" is all you need to say. However, employers will often press you to say whom you're going to work for, just as a rejected suitor might ask if there's someone else. When that happens, how much you share is up to you.

In addition to calling to turn down an offer, you'll also want to follow up with a letter outlining what you mentioned in your conversation. Be sure to thank the recruiter for his or her time and to be complimentary if possible. Your letter should be short and to the point, about the length of a typical thank-you letter you would send after an interview. Figure 9.2 shows a sample.

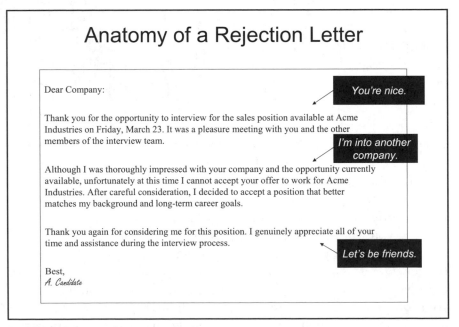

Figure 9.2: Anatomy of a rejection letter.

When the One You Love Is in Love with Someone Else: Bouncing Back When You Don't Get an Offer

Getting dumped can be devastating. When it happens, we're hurt. And when we're hurt, we sometimes want to do stupid things like giving our ex a piece of our mind, calling to say we've gathered up all of his or her belongings and put them out on the front porch in a cardboard box in the rain, or begging for our ex to take us back. I'm sure some of us are even lucky enough to have done them all following one breakup or another.

During your job search, rejection at this stage is practically inevitable. In this situation, as hard as it may be, the last thing you want to do is beg for another chance, lash out and tell the recruiter he or she is making a big mistake, or promise that you can change. This strategy doesn't work when you get dumped by someone you're dating, and it definitely won't work when you get rejected by an employer. All it will do is make you sound desperate and/or crazy and close the door on what little chance you might have of being reconsidered for the position now or in the future.

If you get rejected by a company or organization that seemed likely to hire you, don't take it personally. Any number of factors, including some that were within your control and some that weren't, could have played into the company's decision to pass you over in favor of somebody else. For example, some employers are more interested in candidates they know that other organizations are also looking at. During the interview, they might ask you what other companies you're speaking with. It's a spin on the "it's easier to get a job if you already have a job" concept, where organizations are often more likely to look at candidates who are currently employed at another company than someone who has been unemployed for some time. And it's no different than the often-observed phenomenon that when you start a serious relationship, all of a sudden random people surface who are clamoring for a date with you. Where were these people before you settled down, during those lonely weeks or months?

When you don't receive a job offer, take some time while everything is still fresh in your mind to reflect on the interview process and assess what went wrong and what went right. In most cases, job seekers have a pretty good idea what things they could have done differently, as well as the things they thought went well during an interview. However, the job search isn't always a rational process. In *The Complete Job-Search Handbook,* Howard Figler states, "Sometimes you will be hired when you are not the best candidate (but you got there first), and on other occasions you *are* the best applicant but someone else got hired for some irrelevant reason."[1]

Was It Something That I Said?

To make the most of a rejection, you need to try to gather feedback from organizations that reject you. If you don't, you might end up making the same mistakes over and over. Or, you might guess at what you think went wrong without any way of knowing if your guess was right. For example, if you had 10 first-round interviews with different companies for positions you're qualified for and you didn't get one second-round interview, you could be doing or saying something during the interview that's keeping you from moving on to the second round. But what?

The best way to ask for feedback is to distance yourself from the position for which you were turned down; instead, focus on the fact that you would like general feedback about how you can improve your candidacy for future opportunities. When you use this approach, the person you're speaking with will be more willing to provide general feedback. Plus, if done right, you might also be able to use this encounter as one last chance to pitch why you are the ideal candidate for the opening. Unfortunately, most companies won't share information on your interview performance. Possible reasons that they won't include company policies relating to privacy, possible lawsuits, the time involved, and the potential for confrontation. But it still doesn't hurt to try.

Even though the cards are stacked against you, it takes only one person to give you suggestions that can pay huge dividends. After all, where better to go for feedback about your interview than from the person you interviewed with? Figure 9.3 shows a sample e-mail asking for feedback after getting rejected by an organization. When you're asking for feedback, sending an e-mail is often more effective than calling first because it allows the person you're contacting to gather his or her thoughts before speaking with you over the phone.

---

1. Howard Figler. *The Complete Job-Search Handbook,* Third Edition. New York: Henry Holt and Company, 1999. 295.

Dear Mr. Smith:

I was disappointed to learn that I wasn't selected for the consulting position for which I interviewed on May 10, but I understand how competitive the selection process can be.

I am still very much interested in pursuing a career in the consulting industry and I would greatly appreciate any general feedback or suggestions as to how I can improve my candidacy for future positions.

Please feel free to contact me at your convenience at 555-555-1212. I look forward to hearing from you.

Regards,
Beth Gordon

Figure 9.3: An e-mail requesting feedback after a rejection.

Have a Support Network

As with any stressful time in your life, during your job search, it's a good idea to surround yourself with optimistic people. When you're looking for a job, it's easy to feel insecure, depressed, and overwhelmed at times. The more you can lean on others to help get you through, the better off you'll be. Plus, they'll help you maintain a positive mental attitude, and that will make you a more attractive candidate than someone who is extremely negative.

Keep things in perspective. Remember, just as in the world of dating, there are always other fish in the sea. If things don't work out with one job, there are definitely going to be other opportunities. Take a break to do something you enjoy, something that will help you clear your mind. Sitting around and dwelling on a poor interview or on getting rejected will only hurt your chances of landing a job from future interviews. The more you're able to stay positive and gather feedback from those who didn't make you an offer, the greater your chances of landing a job.

Avoid accepting a job on the rebound. Getting rejected can hurt like hell. It makes you feel vulnerable, damages your self-esteem, and leaves you feeling depressed. Latching onto a job you're not interested in just because you received an offer is the equivalent of dating someone on the rebound. Feeling wanted might feel great, but after you get over the instant gratification of finding a job, chances are you'll realize you were more interested in being wanted by an employer than in the job itself. You can find strategies for helping you to avoid rebounds in the "Getting to Know Yourself" section of chapter 1.

Chapter 10

You've Made Your Match: Job Search Lessons Learned

In courting, as in job seeking, you need to consider your options carefully. As I mentioned earlier, you don't want to wake up one morning wondering how you spent the last 10 years in a dysfunctional relationship or a dead-end job. Invest time in figuring out what you want to do, network, always present yourself in the best possible light, and don't forget to leverage everything you've learned about relationships through your dating experience. Above all else, when you're looking for your next job, always remember to be yourself, relax, and have fun.

Whether you're looking for that special someone or your next job, relationships will have a hand in your success. Just as friends are there to give you dating advice and often try to introduce you to their single friends, others in your social and professional network possess information about industries, career paths, and job openings. But don't forget it's a two-way street. To maintain a healthy relationship, look for ways to help them just as much as you look to them for help.

Know Your Type

Choosing a career is one of the biggest decisions you will make during your lifetime. Don't leave that decision to fate or luck. Start by using some of the self-assessment resources mentioned in chapter 1 to identify your interests, skills, and abilities. After you've completed your self-assessment, take control of your job search by gathering information on careers of interest and developing an effective job search strategy. Do your homework.

Put Yourself Out There

Just as with dating, if your job search is going to be successful, you're going to have to put yourself out there. You're not going to meet that special someone or land that dream job by sitting in front of the television 24 hours a day. Instead, during your job search you'll need to take advantage of the many available resources. Networking, both face-to-face and online, will likely be at the top of your list, as it has historically been *the* most effective method of finding jobs. But don't forget about online posting sites, newspaper ads, company Web sites, staffing agencies, and career fairs.

As your search continues, constantly evaluate the effectiveness of each job search resource and the amount of time you're dedicating to it. If you're having a lot of success with one particular resource, you may want to devote most (but not all) of your energy to that resource.

Always Look Your Best

When you've identified jobs of interest and have interviews lined up, if you're going to ultimately get that job offer, it's critically important that you dress for success and that you adequately prepare for each interview. Just as you would want to look your best on a first date, you also want to make sure you look your best for your interviews. As the saying goes, "You only get one chance to make a first impression." So make it a good one! Wear a conservative suit, polish those dress shoes, and make sure you're properly groomed.

Whether in front of the mirror, in your head, or before you go to sleep at night, visualize your interview. Get comfortable walking someone through your resume. Have your stories down. Review possible interview questions and practice your responses. Be ready to answer the three *whys:* why you're interested in the position, why you're interested in the company, and why the company should hire you instead of someone else. Know a lot about the company. (Of course, that's not a good idea when you're getting ready for a big date.... Can anyone say *stalker?*)

TIP: During your job search, always pay attention to the little things: Avoid typos or other mistakes in your correspondence, dress professionally for interviews, prepare for each and every job or internship interview, send thank-you notes following informational and actual job interviews, and so on. If you don't, all those little things will eventually add up to one big thing: you without a job.

Leverage Your Dating Experience

When times get tough during your job search and you're not sure how to proceed, always try to draw parallels and look for similarities between situations from your job search and from situations you encounter when dating. Doing so will enable you to demystify the job search by looking at it in a context you're more familiar with. Just as not all dates lead to relationships, not all interviews will lead to jobs. There are, and always will be, other fish in the sea.

Go for the Goodnight Kiss

The end of an interview can be just as awkward as the end of a date. You're most likely nervous, asking yourself whether the person you're with wants to give you a romantic goodnight kiss, the "let's be friends" hug, or the always-disappointing "don't call me, I won't call you" handshake. Although you'll never go for a goodnight kiss at the end of an interview, you can still seal the deal by reaffirming your interest in the position and asking about next steps in the interview process.

I wish you the best of luck in courting your career.

Quick Reference

Welcome to your one-stop-shop for a highlight of popular self-assessment resources, helpful career Web sites, career and negotiation worksheets, and sample resumes and cover letters.

Self-Assessment Resources

- **Campbell Interest and Skills Survey (CISS):** Created by Dr. David Campbell, this survey measures self-reported vocational interests and skills. In addition to measuring an individual's attraction to specific occupations, this resource goes beyond other traditional inventories by measuring a person's confidence when performing various occupational activities. Because it examines interests and personal confidence, this survey is more comprehensive than an interest survey alone. The CISS focuses on careers that require a post-secondary education and is used mainly by individuals who are college-bound or those who have a college degree. Completion time: approximately 25 minutes.

- **Temperament Sorter:** This instrument looks at your temperament—your basic personality type—to help you gain a new understanding of your behaviors, traits, and motivations. The Temperament Sorter can help improve self-awareness as well as your understanding of others based on *their* temperaments. I probably don't need to remind you that understanding others is critical, both in dating and on the job. Completion time: approximately 10 minutes.

- **Self-Directed Search (SDS):** Developed by John Holland, the SDS is based on the theory that most people can be loosely categorized with respect to six personality types: Realistic, Investigative, Artistic, Social, Enterprising, and Conventional. Holland believed that occupations and work environments can be classified by the same categories and that people who choose careers that match their personality type are most likely to be satisfied and successful. Completion time: approximately 15 minutes. The **Career Key**, available at www.careerkey.org, is an online adaptation of the SDS and can be helpful in making career choices, accomplishing career changes, or choosing a major. Completion time: approximately 10 minutes.

- **Strong Interest Inventory (Strong):** Based on the concept that individuals are more productive and satisfied when they work in jobs or at tasks they find interesting, the Strong can be used to assist you with a number of issues, such as making career decisions, determining a proper work-life balance, and choosing appropriate training and education. Completion time: approximately 25 minutes.

Popular Career Web Sites

Career Exploration

America's Career Infonet (www.acinet.org/acinet/default.asp)

CareerOverview (www.careeroverview.com)

Occupational Outlook Handbook (www.bls.gov/oco)

O*NET (http://online.onetcenter.org)

Company Research

Hoover's (www.hoovers.com/free/)

Vault (www.vault.com)

WetFeet (www.wetfeet.com)

General Internship Search Engines

InternSearch.com (www.internsearch.com)

InternJobs.com (www.internjobs.com)

InternshipPrograms.com (www.internshipprograms.com)

InternWeb.com (www.internweb.com)

Rising Star Internships (www.rsinternships.com)

Volunteer/Nonprofit

Idealist.org (www.idealist.org)

The Student Conservation Association (www.thesca.org)

VolunteerMatch (www.volunteermatch.org)

Networking Communities

Facebook (www.facebook.com)

Friendster (www.friendster.com)

LinkedIn (www.linkedin.com)

Monster Networking (http://network.monster.com)

MySpace (www.myspace.com)

Ryze (www.ryze.com)

General Job Listing Sites

Indeed (www.indeed.com)

Monster (www.monster.com)

CareerBuilder (www.careerbuilder.com)

Yahoo! HotJobs (http://hotjobs.yahoo.com/)

Industry/Function-Specific Job Listing Sites

Arts and Entertainment

EntertainmentCareers.net
(www.entertainmentcareers.net)

Hollywood Creative Directory
(www.hcdonline.com/jobboard/default.asp)

Museum Jobs (www.museumjobs.com)

Online Sports Career Center
(www.onlinesports.com/pages/CareerCenter.html)

Showbizjobs.com (www.showbizjobs.com)

Business/Finance

Financial Jobs (www.financial-jobs.com)

JobsintheMoney (www.jobsinthemoney.com)

Communications/Media

JournalismJobs.com (www.journalismjobs.com)

Mediabistro.com (www.mediabistro.com/joblistings)

Education

EducationJobs.com (www.educationjobs.com)

K–12Jobs.com (www.k12jobs.com)

Science

BioSpace (http://careers.biospace.com/jobs/Default.aspx)

ScienceJobs.com (www.sciencejobs.com/splash.action)

Technology

ComputerWork.com (www.computerwork.com)

Dice (www.dice.com)

Job Search Sites by Location

BostonJobs.com (www.bostonjobs.com)

ChicagoJobs.com (www.chicagojobs.com)

The New York Job Source (www.nyjobsource.com)

The Washington DC Job Source
(http://dcjobsource.com)

Case Interviews

Bain and Company (www.bain.com)

Boston Consulting Group (www.bcg.com)

Capital One (www.capitalone.com)

McKinsey & Company (www.mckinsey.com)

InterviewPoint
(www.interviewpoint.com/index.php?to=public_index)

Interview Prep

InterviewStream (www.interviewstream.com)

Salary Information

Bureau of Labor Statistics (http://stats.bls.gov/)

CareerJournal.com (www.careerjournal.com/salaryhiring/)

JobStar Central (http://jobstar.org/index.php)

JobWeb (www.jobweb.com/SalaryInfo/default.htm)

Salary.com (www.salary.com)

Salary Expert (www.salaryexpert.com)

Career Management Worksheets

Here are extra copies of the career-management worksheets presented earlier in the book.

Career Wish List

Career area: _____

Likes: _____

_____

_____

_____

Dislikes: _____

_____

_____

_____

Career area: _____

Likes: _____

_____

_____

_____

Dislikes: _____

_____

_____

_____

Name	Title	Organization	Address	City/State/ZIP	Phone	E-mail	Contact Date	Next Steps

Figure A.1: Contact management spreadsheet.

Category	Issue	Force Rank	Personal importance % weight	(Company 1) 1-4 Rating	(Company 1) Wgtd Rating	(Company 2) 1-4 Rating	(Company 2) Wgtd Rating	(Company 3) 1-4 Rating	(Company 3) Wgtd Rating	(Company 4) 1-4 Rating	(Company 4) Wgtd Rating
Career support	Immediate fit with long-term career goal										
Career support	Quality and clarity of available career path through company										
Career support	Training and development emphasis and opportunities										
Job content	Appropriately challenging scope and authority										
Job content	Match to personal competencies, preferences, and development needs (creativity, ambiguity, analytics, technical skills, leadership, etc.)										
Job content	Company resources available to support goals										
Environment	Physical space										
Environment	Access to appropriate technology										
Environment	Amenities and environmental perks										
Environment	Work hours and quality-of-life consideration										
Location	Immediate desirability										
Location	Relocation requirements over time										
Culture	Organizational personality and structure										
Culture	Diversity attitude: encourage, tolerate, discourage? Includes thought as well as physical diversity										
Culture	Decision-making process and style; governance										
Culture	Teamwork style										
Compensation	Salary and bonus										
Compensation	Benefits/perks										
Compensation	Rewards and recognition										
Compensation	Long-term compensation opportunities										
Gut reaction	Passion for company's products or services										
Gut reaction	"I belong here"										
Company	Quality and skill of senior management										
Company	Brand reputation of company/marketability of experience										
Company	Core values										
Company	Quality and skill of immediate supervisor										
Company	Financial condition and direction of firm										
Company	Market strength and prognosis of firm										
Other											
Other											
	TOTALS		100%								

Instructions

1. Decide whether to evaluate the opportunity as a short-term one or for long-term potential.
2. Delete issues of no importance.
3. Add additional issues if needed.
4. Force rank remaining issues, re-sort spreadsheet based on rankings, and assign weights to equal 100%.
5. Rate company(ies) on 1–4 scale (4 = excellent, 1 = poor). Pursue additional information if needed.
6. Add scores.
7. Take final scores into consideration as a factor in decision-making; investigate negotiability of poorly scored items.

Created by, and reprinted with the permission of, Susan Amey
Director of MBA Career Services
UNC's Kenan-Flagler Business School

Figure A.2: Job offer evaluation worksheet.

Sample Action Verbs for Any Resume Format

achieved
addressed
adjusted
advertised
advised
allocated
analyzed
arranged
assembled
assessed
authored
broadened
budgeted
built
calculated
collaborated
collected
communicated
compared
compiled
completed
conceptualized
conducted
consolidated
coordinated
created
defined
delegated
demonstrated
designed
determined
developed
devised
diagnosed
directed
distributed

drafted
enabled
encouraged
established
estimated
evaluated
expanded
expedited
facilitated
forecasted
formulated
generated
guided
headed
hired
identified
illustrated
implemented
improved
increased
influenced
initiated
inspected
instituted
instructed
integrated
interviewed
introduced
invented
launched
lectured
led
liquidated
maintained
managed
marketed

modeled
modified
monitored
motivated
negotiated
obtained
operated
organized
overhauled
oversaw
performed
persuaded
planned
prepared
presented
prioritized
processed
produced
projected
proposed
publicized
recommended
reconciled
recruited
redesigned
referred
reinforced
reorganized
reported
represented
researched
restored
retrieved
reviewed
revised
revitalized

scheduled
served
shaped
simplified
solved
spearheaded
streamlined
strengthened

stretched
structured
studied
supervised
supported
surveyed
taught
tracked

trained
transformed
uncovered
upgraded
utilized
verified
won
wrote

Sample Resumes and Cover Letters

Name
Address
Phone number(s)
E-mail address

OBJECTIVE	Optional. Indicates the type of position for which you are looking; should be concise.
EDUCATION	*YOUR UNIVERSITY* Bachelor of Arts—Your Major, Graduation Month, Year List GPA if 3.0 or higher. Can also list classes if experience is limited.

Study-Abroad University, Seville, Spain   Spring 20XX

EXPERIENCE   *MOST RECENT EMPLOYER*
Your title   Month Year–Month Year
- Describe your experience with phrases and by function.
- Emphasize significant achievements, results produced, and recognition from others.
- Begin phrases with action verbs.
- Quantify accomplishments when possible and use specific examples.

PREVIOUS EMPLOYER
Your title   Month Year Month Year
-
-
-

HONORS   Include academic honors such as scholarships, the Dean's List, and honor societies.

ACTIVITIES
- List offices held, organizations, projects, and skills and abilities utilized.
- Include activities and interests that show leadership or initiative, or Relate to the position for which you are applying.
- Spell out acronyms.

Figure A.3: Resume template.

Katherine Student
1000 Oak Place
Wilson, NC 27896
(919) 555-2400 • Cell: (919) 555-1400
katie.student@unc.edu

EDUCATION

UNIVERSITY OF NORTH CAROLINA AT CHAPEL HILL
School of Journalism and Mass Communication
Bachelor of Arts, May 2008
Public Relations sequence; History minor

EXPERIENCE

REX HEALTHCARE, Raleigh, NC
Public Relations and Marketing Intern, January 2008–May 2008
- Wrote press releases about hospital events, awards, and achievements.
- Assisted marketing coordinators with campaigns for cardiovascular, seniors, and women's health accounts.
- Wrote copy for brochures and fact sheets.
- Communicated directly with local media about press releases and assisted with on-site media events.
- Created surveys to assess the quality of Rex Lactation Services.
- Redesigned RexWebMD and presented revisions to Physician Satisfaction team.

BLUE & WHITE MAGAZINE, UNIVERSITY OF NORTH CAROLINA, Chapel Hill, NC
Publisher, May 2007–February 2008
- Oversaw magazine's financial and business affairs.
- Created a $12,000 budget for the magazine.
- Presented to Student Congress to obtain additional funding for the magazine.

Associate Publisher for Marketing, May 2006–May 2007
- Directed planning of special events, such as a 5K fund-raiser and Student Body President debate.
- Organized distribution of the magazine and other publicity efforts each month.
- Supervised the 10-member marketing team.

Special Events Manager, May 2005–May 2006
- Planned the first *Blue & White* 5K fund-raiser.
- Organized all monthly "pit events" to aid in publicity and distribution of the magazine.
- Created flyers publicizing each new issue of the magazine.

*Communications Assistant—***School of Information and Library Science,** August 2006–May 2007
- Wrote press releases about school-related special events, faculty news, and awards.
- Wrote feature articles about faculty, alumni, and other events for a biannual alumni newsletter.
- Updated School of Information and Library Science website, www.ils.unc.edu.

WILSON DAILY TIMES, Wilson, NC
News Intern, August 2002–January 2006
- Wrote three to five stories weekly for a newspaper serving approximately 30,000 readers.
- Awarded "Best Story of the Quarter" for a feature story.
- Wrote two articles accepted by The Associated Press and published in seven newspapers throughout North Carolina.

COMPUTER
SKILLS

Proficient: Microsoft Word, Works, Excel, and PowerPoint
Knowledgeable: HTML, Dreamweaver, and Photoshop

Figure A.4: Sample chronological resume.

JOHN STUDENT
jstudent@email.unc.edu

SCHOOL ADDRESS: HOME ADDRESS:
107 Pritchard Avenue   1000 Buhl Avenue
Chapel Hill, NC 27516   Memphis, TN 38104
919.555.1111   901.555.2222

EDUCATION   *UNIVERSITY OF NORTH CAROLINA AT CHAPEL HILL*
                     Bachelor of Arts in History, May 2008
                     Cumulative GPA: 3.32

HONORS   Dean's List
                     Sigma Chi Alumni Scholarship—all semesters

EXPERIENCE   *ACME TRAFFIC SERVICES*, Chapel Hill, NC
                     Co-Owner and Operator, Fall 2006–Spring 2008
                     • Started a business projected to gross over $10,000 in first year of operation.
                     • Maintained accurate accounting records for tax and payroll purposes.
                     • Marketed business to potential clients.
                     • Successfully completed engagements, securing repeat customers.
                     • Set up a branch site in Memphis, TN, under a commission paid employee.

                     GTX, INC., Memphis, TN
                     Financial Assistant, Summers 2006–2007
                     • Assisted in documentation to support private financing rounds.
                     • Exposed to the process of preparing for a biotech initial public offering
                     • Participated in development of cash-flow forecasts using Excel.

                     Lab Technician, Summer 2005
                     • Compiled data from an experiment testing an viral implication.
                     • Calibrated instruments for Quality Assurance analysis.

LEADERSHIP   *SIGMA CHI FRATERNITY*, Chapel Hill, NC
EXPERIENCE   **Social Chairman,** Fall 2006–Spring 2007
                     • Controlled a $12,000 budget each semester and coordinated events.

                     Intramural Chairman, Fall 2004–Spring 2006
                     • Secured participation of 60 members for 10 intramural sports.

CAMPUS   *Carolina Entrepreneurial Club*
ACTIVITIES   *Dance Marathon*
                     Intramural Sports

COMPUTER   Microsoft Word, Excel, PowerPoint, QuickBooks
SKILLS

Figure A.5: Sample chronological resume.

STEVEN M. SMITH
34 Clayton Road
Concord, CA 94520
925-555-5555
ssmith237@excite.net

SKILLS

MANAGEMENT
- Supervised and scheduled a staff of approximately 50 employees.
- Resolved and documented all employee personnel issues.
- Conducted sanitation and safety inspections to ensure department meets or exceeds JCAHO standards.
- Developed and conducted training and in-services for all departmental staff.
- Participated in interviewing, hiring, performance evaluations, and termination of employees.
- Monitored and maintained departmental inventory levels.

COMMUNICATION
- Created and enforced Dietary Department policies and procedures.
- Planned and prepared menus for special events.
- Prepared and submitted financial reports.
- Counseled patients on drug-nutrient interactions.
- Conducted general health and nutritional information seminars for community members.

CUSTOMER SERVICE
- Ensured high level of customer satisfaction by providing prompt, friendly service.
- Interacted with sales representatives, doctors, and other constituencies.

EXPERIENCE

CONTRA COSTA REGIONAL MEDICAL CENTER, Martinez, CA
Assistant Director of Nutritional Services   12/06–Present

LONE TREE CONVALESCENT HOSPITAL, Antioch, CA
Dietary Supervisor   4/04–12/06

UNIVERSITY OF PITTSBURGH MEDICAL CENTER, Farrell, PA
Nutritional Services Team Leader   5/03–3/04
Dietetic Technician   9/99–5/03

EDUCATION

YOUNGSTOWN STATE UNIVERSITY, Youngstown, OH   9/01–3/02
Master of Science courses—Health and Human Services
Accounting and Science courses

INDIANA UNIVERSITY OF PENNSYLVANIA, Indiana, PA   1999
Bachelor of Science—Dietetics
Concentration—Hotel, Restaurant, and Institutional Management

LEADERSHIP

Safety Committee Chairman, Lone Tree Convalescent Hospital
Member, UPMC Horizon Quality Improvement Team

Figure A.6: Sample combination resume.

Your street address
City, State ZIP
Month, date, year

[2 spaces]

Recruiter's name
Title
Company
Street address
City, State Zip
[1 space]
Dear Mr./Ms./Dr._____:
[1 space]
Opening paragraph: Start your letter with a brief introduction, including the name of the position you are applying for. If you've had prior conversations with people at the company or attended a recent recruiting event they held on or off campus, mention that here. You should also highlight the reasons you're interested in working for their company rather than one of their competitors. A strong opening paragraph grabs the reader's attention.
[1 space]
Second/Third paragraphs: The body of your cover letter should focus on how your skills and experience match those of what they're looking for in a candidate. Review the job description and highlight content from your resume that will spark the reader's interest. If you have limited experience, focus on coursework and leadership roles. Show you've done your homework and that you know about the company by incorporating information about them in your cover letter.
[1 space]
Closing paragraph: Reiterate your interest in the company and the position and indicate a desire to interview for the position. Indicate next steps (for example, I will contact you in...). Include your phone number and e-mail and offer your assistance in the event they need additional information.
[1 space]
Thank the reader for his or her time.
[1 space]
Sincerely,
[3 spaces] (Your handwritten signature)
(Your name typed)
[1 space]
Enclosure (denotes resume, applications, etc. that are enclosed)

Figure A.7: Sample cover letter.

1 River Crossing Drive
Chapel Hill, NC 27517
(Date)

Mr. Phillip Jones
Institutional Sales, Equities Division
Acme Securities
100 East 14th Street
New York, NY 10004

Dear Mr. Jones:

I am writing to express my interest in interviewing for a position in Equity Research. I was highly impressed with Acme Securities' presentations to Big State University this fall. I also enjoyed meeting with your colleagues when I visited New York City in November.

I am familiar with Acme Securities' excellent reputation and consistently strong ranking in Equity Research. Also, lead managing 14 successful initial public offerings this year is evidence of your firm's strong culture and ability to succeed during difficult economic conditions. This has heightened my desire to work for Acme Securities.

Over the last five years, I have worked in financial institution mergers and acquisitions. Some of my accomplishments during this period include receiving the CFA designation, creating an equity research product for thinly traded banks, and managing multiple bank and thrift transactions. While pursuing my MBA, I continue to be employed as an independent financial consultant. I have worked hard over this period to develop my skills in anticipation of pursuing an Equity Research position following graduate school.

I have enclosed a copy of my resume for your review. If you have any further questions regarding my qualifications, please do not hesitate to contact me at 919-555-5555.

Thank you for your time and consideration.

Respectfully,

Alex Applicant

Alex Applicant, CFA

Enclosure

Figure A.8: Sample cover letter.

References

Hunt, Kimberly N. *Encyclopedia of Associations: National Organizations of the U.S.* Farmington Hills: Thomson Gale, 2004.

U.S. Department of Labor. *Occupational Outlook Handbook.* Indianapolis: JIST Publishing, 2006.

Index

X–Z